Here's W

"SAY GRACE gives us tools and truths straight from the Gospel to help us walk lighter and get off the "treadmill of performance" that we so often live on. This book reminds us of the freedom we have through Jesus Christ. Jeff is honest and convicting, helping us understand that personally micromanaging our sin gets us nowhere. However, living fully redeemed and free in Christ gets us everywhere!"

Candace Cameron Bure
"FULLER HOUSE", "THE VIEW"

"Jeff Taylor has been a partner of ours in ministry for many years. His transparency and vulnerability have made him a special kind of radio personality who connects with people in a way that has little to do with entertainment and everything to do with ministry. SAY GRACE is a book that speaks to the brokenness in all of us. And it celebrates God's amazing grace - grace that forgives and transforms lives! This book will rock your world because that's what the Gospel does. Take the journey, mates!"

Joel and Luke
FOR KING & COUNTRY

"I've known Jeff Taylor for years now, and have often been encouraged by his words on God's overwhelming and relentless grace and forgiveness. In SAY GRACE, Jeff takes this message to a whole new level and holds nothing back. His writing is raw, transparent and honest. It is a timely and powerful reminder of how intensely radical Gods love is for us. Even when life gets messy and we're at our very worst, Gods grace covers all!"

Josh Havens
THE AFTERS

"Like a cup of cool water on a hot day, SAY GRACE offers the refreshment of the Gospel to weary souls"

Rev. Pat Thurmer
PASTOR, LIVING FAITH CHURCH,
Cape Coral, Florida

"SAY GRACE will most likely raise some initial objections from Christian readers. We are used to settling for a three-point sermon about how we can be more successful at managing our sin, and appearing reasonably holy. Jeff Taylor makes us reexamine how amazing 'amazing grace' is. Jesus died for SINNERS. This deeply offends our inner Pharisee. But our inner Prodigal sees God running toward us, arms open with love. Read this."

Randy Thomas
GRAMMY-WINNING SONGWRITER
"BUTTERFLY KISSES"
ALLIES, SWEET COMFORT BAND

"Everything is broken. Jeff knows this. From his own life and struggles he is a man who knows the reality of brokenness through the things he does and the things that have been done to him. And yet, brokenness is not the last word of his, or anyone's story. Grace is. Grace that transforms our brokenness into something beautiful because of Jesus. Jeff lives this out in his own life as a flawed but loved child of God and friend of Jesus, and now, as an author for the rest of us to learn to trust and follow Jesus whose grace only flows downhill. Read this book, enjoy it, but more importantly, follow Jeff's lead through it in making much of Jesus, not yourself."

Chris Gensheer
LEAD PASTOR, CHRIST CHURCH,
Mansfield, TX (PCA)

say grace
40 Days Of Good News

Jeff Taylor Sandnes

Scripture quotations are from The ESV® Bible (The Holy Bible, English Standard Version®), copyright © 2001 by Crossway, a publishing ministry of Good News Publishers. Used by permission. All rights reserved.

Scripture quotations are taken from the Holy Bible, New Living Translation, copyright ©1996, 2004, 2007, 2013, 2015 by Tyndale House Foundation. Used by permission of Tyndale House Publishers, Inc., Carol Stream, Illinois 60188. All rights reserved.

Copyright © 2017 I Am Broken

ISBN 978-0-692-93746-4

All rights reserved. No part of this publication may be reproduced, stored in a retrieval system, or transmitted in any form or by any means, electronic, mechanical, photocopy, recording or otherwise, without permission of the author. Printed in the United States of America.

Layout by Penoaks Publishing, http://penoaks.com

This book is dedicated to my daughter Kate Olivia.

There hasn't been a word invented that could adequately describe the love I feel for her. She and I have a very special relationship and I think it has something to do with the fact that we're so much alike. But she looks like her mom, thankfully!

She's not like most other kids and her gifts and talents are unique. Her creativity amazes me and I love watching her on the theater stage. Kate is so gifted!

But what makes me so proud is the fact that she has such a heart for the Lord. She, too, has been captivated by the Gospel! Kate is trusting in Christ and His finished work and she understands grace better than most adults I know. And that grace is transforming her life. It's so fun to watch her grow in Christ.

I have let her down so many times and she forgives me always. I have failed to be the dad she deserves and yet she lavishes me with gracious love. She is God's gift to me and I'm so thankful that I get to call her MY daughter!

I'm here for you always, Libby Lu...

Love, Dad

contents

Introduction	iii
1: Yep, I'm One Of The Broken Ones...	1
2: This Is Where A Lot Of Us Get It Wrong	5
3: The Math Of The Mind Vs. The Chemistry Of The Heart	9
4: Lessons From The Uneven Bars...	13
5: Marching Orders? I Don't Think So...	17
6: "Let's NOT Make A Deal!"	21
7: We Are Josh Duggar!	25
8: The Sin We Can't Forget...	29
9: A Change Of Identity	33
10: "I Could Never Believe In A God Who Could Forgive Someone Like Me..."	37
11: Are You Getting It Done?	41
12: Just Tell Me What I Have To Do!	45
13: The Tandem Jumper I Need To Be...	49
14: Fathers And Their Children	53
15: A Safe Place To Fall...	57
16: "This Is My Beloved Son, In Whom I Am Well-Pleased!"	61
17: I Am Truly The Worst Man In America!	65
18: Yes, Grace...But What About OBEDIENCE?	69
19: Regarding Henry...	73

20: I Get By With A Little Help…	77
21: A Picture Of Grace That Might Offend You…	81
22: You Need More Than A Second Chance, You Know…	85
23: You're More Desperate Than You Think…	89
24: Theology Of Glory Vs. Theology Of The Cross	94
25: I'm Not Sure I'd Pass That Test…	98
26: Stop Trying To Have A Relationship With God!	102
27: Jim Carrey Gets It!	106
28: Reputations	110
29: But Why Did He Have To DIE?	115
30: What Are You Trying To Accomplish?	119
31: The Perfect Church	123
32: My Story	127
33: It's The Bomb-Diggity!	131
34: Meet Me Halfway?	135
35: The Aggressive Pursuer	139
36: "You Can't Handle The Truth!"	143
37: Jesus Is NOT "The Reason For The Season"!	147
38: "Oh, Come On, You're Not That Bad…"	151
39: The Broken Ones Are Over There…	155
40: "That Camper You're Pulling Is Really Gonna Slow You Down!"	159
Stuff I Forgot To Say…	163
Sources	167
Meet Jeff Taylor Sandnes	172

acknowledgements

I would like to thank so many people who helped to make *Say Grace* a reality.

My family was so encouraging during the writing of this book. They wanted me to write it even more than I did, and I'm grateful for their support. Many hours watching dad at the computer and always an encouraging word…

Brad Buckles, who served as the primary copy editor for *Say Grace*, gave me tremendous help! His ideas are all over the book and I'm so grateful for his friendship.

KCBI in Dallas-Ft. Worth has given me a place to tell these stories to 400,000 people every day. We're doing some fun work there and I'm honored to be a part. Matt Austin, Sharon Geiger and Joel Burke have given me a freedom to share my brokenness on the air I couldn't have imagined. Thank you.

Rebecca Carrell and I talk about the beauty of God's grace all the time and she's been such a gift to me. My family calls her my "work wife" and she's one of my dearest friends.

Tullian Tchividjian and his writings changed my life. Thank you, sir, for helping me to put the ladder away and marvel at the Cross. You inspired so much of this book.

And to the One who loves me most and loves me best – thank you Jesus! You took my name with you to Calvary and I rest in your work. Thank you for new life…

introduction

This book is personal for me. I've written it in hopes that over the course of forty days, God's message of radical grace will captivate you. MY words will never ever captivate you. But the Gospel has the power to grip your heart and life, changing you to the core. The good news that Jesus loves broken and messed up sinners is something that most Christians believe. But the reality that His redemptive work means that we will never face God's condemnation – not ever – is hard for some of us to believe.

We like to add stuff to the message of the Cross. We place conditions on the Gospel that make the whole thing sound like a lot of work on our part. We attach requirements that cannot be found in the Bible.

I was driving across Montana in the middle of the night and I was in the middle of nowhere trying to find a radio station to tune into. There was only one – a Christian radio station. Chuck Swindoll was speaking and he said something that rocked my world. He said that for the Christian it isn't Jesus + commitment. Nor was it Jesus + dedication. It wasn't Jesus + promises. And it certainly wasn't Jesus + devotion. None of that could save us. Chuck said, "It's Jesus, Jesus, Jesus!!!"

Tullian Tchividjian, who is Billy Graham's grandson, said something once that really resonated with me. He said, "My grandfather is an evangelist for people outside the church. I am an evangelist for people inside the church!"

That's sort of become my mantra. I speak to 400,000 people on the radio each week and most of them are people of faith. Many of them are weary and worn out because of all the conditions that have been placed on the gospel that they can't possibly meet. I share the simple message of grace on our show because we all need to hear it! We need to be liberated by it. We need to preach it to ourselves every day lest we go back to believing that our standing with God is anchored in our improvement as Christians.

My prayer is that as you soak in the good news over forty days, things will change for you. I hope that you will be set free from what Tchividjian calls "performancism". There is nothing more that you need to do to secure His love for you. Just believe and receive! And as you open your heart to a message that might fly in the face of all you've heard in church growing up, God will give you comfort, relief and rest. It really is finished. He died once, for all. And when the truth of that sinks in, you will experience joy in your life like never before because the chains are really off – for good! You can breathe.

You can love and serve Him, not out of obligation, but from a place of gratitude. This journey will hurt at times. None of us wants to face the ugly reality of our sin. We do that in this book. But once we've let the Law slay us, the good news of the Gospel is that much sweeter! It will become GOOD NEWS!! And it will change your life. It will reorient you and you will read the Bible differently. You will see that the whole book is about Jesus and not us.

Read. Enjoy. Breathe. The news is really good, you see…

Please allow me to give shout out to some of the men and women who have been voices of grace in my life. Find their books and blogs. Read them! You'll be blessed as I have been. Thank you to Scotty Smith, Ray Ortlund, Bryan Chapell, Steve Brown, Elyse Fitzpatrick, Brennan Manning, Matt Chandler, Jessica Thompson, Paul Tripp, Tim Keller, Gerhard Forde, Brad Soenksen, Rick Bridston, Orlando Cabrera, Jamin Stinziano, Brad Hoganson, Jorge Acevedo, Ed Nugent, Pat Thurmer, David Christenson, Chris Gensheer, Rebecca Carrell and my pastor Greg Buckles.

1

Yep, I'm One Of The Broken Ones...

I will never forget the shame I felt when my wife came into the bedroom where I was trying to get to sleep and asked me some simple question. I sounded like a fool because my answer was slurred and made little sense. I was drunk. She caught me and I was mortified. It wouldn't have been a big deal except I'm an alcoholic and as far as she knew I wasn't drinking anymore. The shame and regret that I felt in that moment is hard to describe and painful to relive. I had to confess to Larisa that I had wrongly reintroduced alcohol into my life and needed help. Confession is a good thing, but it really hurts in that moment. Was she going to kick me out of the house? Would she take the kids and leave me to deal with this alone?

I had been found out and it hurt! More about that later in the book.

The bad news for you and me today is this: We've been found out! As much as we've tried to fool those around us, the reality of our brokenness has been exposed…by God. He knows all of it. He's even more aware of how messed up we are than we are! It's true. Our failures and flaws, our rebellion and secret sins – He knows every part of it.

He knows how broken we really are. We think we know the degree to which we are broken, but we are so unaware of much that's wrong with us. He knows us and knows ALL of our junk.

In John 4, Jesus is with a Samaritan woman at a well. They have a brief exchange about how they shouldn't be socializing because she is, in fact a Samaritan.

He begins to tell her about Living Water and she says, "Give me a drink!" Then Jesus begins to peel away the mask that she was wearing…

Jesus said to her, "Go, call your husband, and come here." The woman answered him, "I have no husband." Jesus said to her, "You are right in saying, 'I have no husband'; for you have had five husbands, and the one you now have is not your husband. What you have said is true." John 4:16-18 ESV

I don't think that Jesus was trying to shame her, but rather, He wanted her to know that He was God in human flesh. He could see below the surface to all the things that she was ashamed of – all of her failures and sin. I bet it stung to be found out in that moment. It always hurts to have our mess exposed. It brings shame, regret and embarrassment.

God knows how truly messed up we are and He calls us out on it. In fact, our sin is so bad that it makes us God's enemies! Our sin sickens Him and deserves to be dealt with. Whether you're a church elder or a serial killer, your sin deserves incredible punishment…and so does mine. But God chose to punish another. He punished His Son Jesus who took full and final responsibility for your sin and mine. All of it! He absorbed every bit of God's holy wrath – the wrath that we deserved because of our sin. God looked at His Son on the cross and basically said, "You make me SICK!"

I know how vulgar that sounds, but it is true. In that moment on the Cross, God turned His back on His beloved Son allowing Him to take our sin upon His shoulders.

The Bible is clear about what Jesus' death accomplished for you and me:

"For God made Christ, who never sinned, to be the offering for our sin so that we could be made right with God through Christ." 2 Corinthians 5:21 NLT

Think about the implications of that truth for you and me today! We've been found out!! Exposed for the sinful frauds that we are. Sick with sin and guilty under God's holy Law. But Jesus took our place. And not only did He take responsibility for all of our sin – past, present and future, He credits us with His perfect righteousness!! The burden of our sin has been lifted and now we are free!

But some of us struggle to believe that it's really true! It's almost like we're afraid of this freedom. Why would we be? I think that it's simply a reflection of how messed up our thinking has gotten because of sin. We desperately want to believe it's true, but somehow we don't dare. I wrote this little book to remind you that you can believe in the Gospel because it is absolutely true for YOU! His blood was poured out for YOU! He stood in your place.

Brennan Manning knew brokenness very well:

> *"To be alive is to be broken; to be broken is to stand in need of grace."*[1]

What does this mean? It means that when it comes to our condition, there are no superior ones. No one enters this world in an unbroken state. No one is less broken than anyone else. And we are far more broken and messed up than we can even imagine. Yet because of Christ's finished work, we are now seen by God as though we were Jesus himself.

As you navigate through this day, you will be tempted to think that although God poured out His wrath on Jesus, He's saving a little for you because you're THAT messed up. It's a lie. Because the Gospel is true, you can walk in freedom today. God is no longer angry with you. Jesus won for you God's 100% acceptance and love.

Walk a little lighter today knowing that you can't do anything to mess this up!

a prayer for today

Thank you, God, for your faithfulness when I am faithless. Your voice is the one I need to hear above all the others today. I will be tempted to doubt your love and acceptance because when I fail and fall today, I will feel shame and regret. But you promise forgiveness and grace and mercy - the stuff I need to go on. Please help me to find rest in you today.

2
This Is Where A Lot Of Us Get It Wrong

One of the greatest traps that we as believers fall into is this: SIN MANAGEMENT. We spend our day trying to minimize our sins, while at the same time, working at behaving better. On the surface, this sounds really good and spiritual. We read the "don'ts" of the Bible and we try with all our might to stop doing those things. And a lot of us who've gone through seasons of sin management have been left feeling weary, worn out and discouraged. We also live in fear that because we haven't gotten rid of ALL those sinful things in our lives, God is frustrated with us.

My brother-in-law, who is a pastor and a really smart guy, told a powerful story that gave me a new perspective on my sin and my need.

Once upon a time, there was a farmer who had a small plot of land with a field that was not producing good crop. As he looked at his field he noticed that there were rocks everywhere. He thought, "If I can get rid of these rocks then crops will grow!" He began picking rocks out of his field.

The more rocks he picked, the more seemed to show up. He literally spent years picking rocks out of his farm field. After many years of rock-picking, he realized that he had gotten every single rock out of the field. He was both exhausted and elated because his hard work had paid off! His field was free of all the rocks that prevented crop growth.

What this hard-working, well-intended farmer didn't know is that his entire field sat on a bedrock.

Over time, the rock that his field sat on would slowly push more and more rocks to the surface. There was no way that he could possibly pick out enough rocks to clear out his field over the long haul.

Do you see where I'm going? As believers, so many of us spend our spiritual energy trying to pick the sins out of our lives. Why do we do it? Maybe we do it out of fear – like God will turn His back on us if we're not getting rid of our bad behaviors. Some of us do it because we think that it was Jesus' blood and sweat that got us in, but it is going to be our blood and sweat that KEEPS us in!

I talk to people all the time who find themselves toiling in sin management. They think that if they succeed in their quest to rid their lives of all the bad stuff, God will certainly approve of them because of their hard work. They are spiritual rock pickers who pride themselves on their ability to get better. But in every case they are exhausted and hopeless when they find out that there is more sin in their lives than they ever imagined. They are sin-soaked! And still, in their weariness, they keep picking rocks, as though their standing with God is dependent on it.Sin management will only leave us exhausted, discouraged and afraid.

And yet, in pulpits everywhere, pastors are preaching a message that seemingly flies in the face of the Gospel. Many churches have become places where sinners learn how to be better behaved. Virtue and integrity are the goals. This moralistic mess has given birth to people who have been brought up to do lots of good Christian things, but are not hearing the good news that in Christ we are the righteousness of God! Obedience is seen as a means to an end.

And this kind of message is being shoved down the throats of our youth all the time! We emphasize character and not brokenness. We champion good kids who don't do all the bad stuff. That's not entirely a bad thing, unless it's devoid of a Gospel context. Grace is seen as something that will just give kids license to live any way they want.

But for those of us who are in Christ – who are trusting in the finished work of Jesus – we are called to rest in the Gospel!

We recognize that our best efforts to get better only exposed the greater depth of our sin problem.

And sin management also creates another problem for you and me. The more we feel like we're "getting it right" and eliminating our bad behaviors, the more self-righteous we become. And with self-righteousness comes a judgmental spirit.

Today, you and I will be tempted to believe that God is measuring our improvement and watching carefully to see how many rocks we can pick out of our farm field. You can live this way but it will undoubtedly leave you weary and discouraged because you will never get it done. And you'll be tempted to think that your standing with God is based on how you're doing at sin management. Don't believe it! It's a lie from the pit of hell. If you're in Christ, you are loved and accepted because of the work of Jesus on your behalf.

What will happen for you as you trust in Him and His finished work is this: The Holy Spirit will begin to reproduce the character of Christ in you. And while you continue to fail and fall and doubt and struggle, you are covered by Jesus' blood, redeemed forever! And like I say often in this book: You can't do anything to mess that up! Your standing with Him is secure because of what He has done to make things right!

What will this good news mean for you today?

a prayer for today

God, thank you that I don't have to begin this day with a clean slate. If I did, I would have to live with the pressure to "get it done" today, filling that clean slate with my best stuff for the day. Thanks, Lord, that my slate is filled with Jesus' righteousness. There's nothing for me to add to it. It's full. No gaps. Help me, God, to walk in the freedom that this good news provides. May this simple truth change my heart today.

3
The Math Of The Mind Vs. The Chemistry Of The Heart

I often say that if grace doesn't sound too good to be true, then you haven't heard about grace. People sometimes respond by telling me that grace is fine as long as you "don't go too far with it." The fear is that grace will produce lazy Christians who simply live their lives any way they want. They are concerned that people who really believe in the radicality of God's grace will abuse the freedom that they are given through the Gospel. Maybe you feel the same way…

What I have discovered for myself is this: The more I soak in the radical truth of Jesus' unmerited favor given to great sinners like me, the more I want to serve Him! The more I hear about God's love for me, sending His Son to die in my place, the more I am wowed and wooed by it. Rather than producing a laziness in me, it creates a desire to know the One who loves me!

Years ago I attended a conference called LIBERATE. It was three days of nothing but Good News! The first night, a seminary professor named Bryan Chapell spoke about the tension that exists where the Gospel is championed.

He said it this way:

> *"The Math of The Mind says that because the Gospel is true, I can live my life any way I want and God will make it right in the end."*

Truthfully, I've seen this play out in the lives of people I know. It makes me sad to think that anyone would approach life in Christ this way. I even wonder if this person truly believes the Gospel. But Chapell continues:

> *"But The Chemistry of the Heart says, 'If He loves me THAT MUCH, then I want to please Him...'"*

A few years ago, when the Gospel truly captivated me, I found myself so amazed at what Jesus had done for me that I wanted to serve Him with my life. Not so that I would get something more from Him, but because the Holy Spirit had begun to cultivate a heart of gratitude for the grace that I had been given.

Zaccheus understood this.

When Jesus passed through town and called out to the tax collector Zacchaeus who was in a sycamore tree saying,

"Zacchaeus, come down for I must stay at your house today!" Luke 19:5b NLT

The crowd grumbled because they knew the dishonest jerk that Zacchaeus was. I'm sure they all thought that he should be the last man to receive kindness from Jesus, given his reputation. And yet, Zacchaeus was so blown away at Jesus' gesture of unexpected love he responded:

"Behold, Lord, the half of my goods I give to the poor. And if I have defrauded anyone I restore it FOURFOLD!" Luke 19:8 NLT

Jesus demanded nothing from Zacchaeus, but rather, showed him extravagant love. And a broken sinner's life was changed forever. This is what happens when the Gospel reaches into your brokenness and announces that if you believe, you are forviven and free – free to love and serve Him with no conditions attached. The heart that has truly been set free wants to love the lover back!

You see, it's the love of Jesus that compels us to good works. It inspires them and it produces them in the lives of the believer. As we marinate in God's radical love for broken sinners like us, something amazing happens: We begin to live our lives in a new way, reoriented by the Gospel!

This is precisely why I have written this little book. My hope is that if you spend 40 days soaking in the good news of God's grace for broken sinners like us, it will change your heart and life! You could listen to a podcast or watch a YouTube video from a lot of folks who can tell you how to have a life of fulfillment and purpose. That's NOT the Gospel! We sinners need a healthy dose of good news every day. My prayer for you and for me is that today we would let the Chemistry of the Heart overtake the Math of the Mind in your life. Who knows what might happen? If your experience is like mine, you will find yourself wanting to love and serve Him with your life as an act of love, born out of the incredible gratitude that the Gospel creates within us. And it will become spontaneous!

Allow the sweet news of His extravagant love for you to wash over you, again and again. And watch what happens in your heart and mind…

a prayer for today

God, I wish I could start this day with a promise to "keep you #1 in my life", to "serve you with unbridled passion", and to "give you every area of my life". But if I make that promise, I will break it over and over again today. Thanks for the grace and mercy that you pour into the lives of faithless people like me. You are faithful and you promise to hold on to me when my grip fails. Thanks for loving me today…

4
Lessons From The Uneven Bars...

As I said earlier, I spent the better part of my life believing that it was Jesus' blood and sweat that GOT me in, but it was my blood and sweat that would KEEP me in. This put me on what one writer calls "The Treadmill of Performance". I was living under the weight of a theology that said, "Do more, try harder!" There would be no resting, relaxing, nor any real peace because I lived in fear that if I died suddenly, I might not have done enough to be right with God.

I read in Galatians about freedom in Christ but I certainly felt none at all. I believed in a God who loved me, saved me but was now micromanaging my life.

When I was young, I played little league baseball. My coach was Charlie. He was a nice guy and everyone I knew liked him. That's because they didn't have to play baseball for him. He was a yeller and a screamer. It's amazing I survived that year of "fun"!

I was a first-baseman and I was not particularly talented. I tried really hard but I prayed to God that no balls would be hit in my direction! Charlie was hard on me. The more he yelled at me, the more errors I made. I was wound up so tight that I could hardly function out there in the field. His coaching style robbed me of any and all joy in playing the game. I lived in fear, and it really messed me up.

One day at practice, Charlie was riding me for not playing well and something wild happened. I snapped! I started yelling back at him, crying, with spit flying as I exploded at my coach. I told him what he was doing to me and I sounded like a crazy man as I did!!

There was no joy in playing baseball for me that year. None at all. I felt like Charlie was watching me with eyes that wanted me to fail. He made it impossible for me to relax and enjoy.

For years, I looked at God the same way. In my mind, God was generally annoyed with my progress as His follower. He was watching and waiting to remind me that because He sent Jesus for me I needed to get my Christian act together or He would eventually kick me to the curb. I was a "lukewarm Christian" at best!

It wasn't until I was 42 years old that the gospel came alive in me. I experienced the liberating power of the gospel.

In Galatians 5 we read, **"For freedom Christ has set us free; stand firm therefore, and do not submit again to a yoke of slavery." Galatians 5:1 ESV**

So how do free people live? What does the free life look like for broken people who have had their chains removed? If there is no longer the possibility of condemnation for the believer, how then do we respond to the Savior, who gives us grace upon grace? I have an idea…

In 2012, I was watching the US Women's Gymnastics Olympic Trials. I love gymnastics, you see. As the team seemed to be coming together, I was curious to see how Nastia Liukin would do.

I watched her four years earlier as she won Gold in the 2008 Olympic Individual All-Around. Now, four years later, she was simply hoping to make the team. It was on the uneven bars that her dream of another Olympic games came to an end.

She was hoisted onto the high bar by her father and coach. As she began swinging it was obvious that she wasn't the same athlete that had won Gold in 2008. Early in her routine she attempted a release move and when she reached for the bar, it wasn't there. She fell to the mat flat on her face. It was over. She wouldn't qualify for the games.

But instead of walking away, she jumped up on the bars and started to swing. She didn't care about her score. She simply swung on the bars because she loved to do it. It was for the joy of being a gymnast, without care for her score that she swung. When her routine ended she paid no attention to the score. She walked away with joy because she did what she loved. And her father was never more proud.

What does freedom in Christ look like? It looks like that! We swing on the bars simply because we love to do it. And Jesus achieved for us a perfect 10!! So now we are free to swing…and even fall, because our Heavenly Father loves to watch His children live without the burden of a score.

Steve Brown articulates this idea of freedom in Christ better than anyone I've ever heard:

> *"What does it mean to be free in Christ? It means we are free from the rules we thought bound us to God. It means we are free from the manipulation other Christians use to make us like them—free from having to fit into the world's mold, free to be different. We are free from the slavery of religion and from the fear of rejection, alienation, and guilt. We are free from the fear of death. We are free from masks, free from the sham and pretense; free to doubt, free to risk, free to question. It means we are free to live every moment. But most of all, we are free to follow Christ, not because we have to but because we want to."* [1]

We are free to live and breathe and experience lives that are a response to the God who loves us. No fear of falling and failing! Our "Daddy" loves to watch us walk in freedom! He really does. The score sheets and ledgers have been thrown out. Our Judgment Day has been moved from the future to the past! We are free to experience life in Christ! Wow!

Go swing on the bars today! And don't fear...

a prayer for today

Lord, please give me the joy that comes from knowing that I'm your child! Help me to rest in the truth of your Word today. God, it's exhausting to think that I have to do something to earn your love and acceptance. That's a load I can't bear. Thank you for the Gospel that announces your finished work. Help me to live this day with the assurance that comes from your promise to never leave me. Remind me that there's nothing I can do to fall out of favor with you.

5
Marching Orders? I Don't Think So...

When we read the words of Jesus in the Sermon On The Mount, many of us read them and hear the wrong message. And if we do, the truth of the Gospel can get lost.

In Matthew 5-7, Jesus preaches a powerful message. But if we are to understand the context of this passage, we have to know who Jesus was speaking to. The Jews that gathered to hear Jesus were oh so familiar with the Law of Moses. They made it their mission to keep that law. They took great pride in observing and obeying the commands given to them. I imagine that many of them felt a sense of self-righteousness because they were, in their minds, getting it done.

In the Sermon On The Mount, Jesus restates many of the 10 Commandments for His audience. He often begins each point by refencing the Law saying, "You have heard it said…" But He then restates the Law by ratcheting up the expectations:

"You have heard that it was said to those of old, 'You shall not murder; and whoever murders will be liable to judgment.' But I say to you that everyone who is angry with

his brother will be liable to judgment; whoever insults his brother will be liable to the council; and whoever says, 'You fool!' will be liable to the hell of fire. You have heard that it was said, 'You shall not commit adultery.' But I say to you that everyone who looks at a woman with lustful intent has already committed adultery with her in his heart. You have heard that it was said, 'You shall love your neighbor and hate your enemy.' But I say to you, Love your enemies and pray for those who persecute you." Matthew 5:21-22; 27-28; 43-44

I believe He gave these words, not to offer marching orders to the crowd, but rather, to SLAY those who believed that they were getting it done. How could anyone hear His words that day and feel good about themselves? These were people who thought that they were getting it done. Their success in this life had everything to do with their meeting of God's holy expectations. For those who really felt like they were keeping the Law, they must have felt crushed.

I think Jesus wanted it that way. He wanted them to know that they had been found out!

The Good News of the Gospel doesn't sound that great until the Law has crushed you. Only when we acknowledge how far from God's expectations we are can we really be amazed at the grace given to us in Christ. The bible says that even our best works are "like filthy rags" because they are tainted by our sin.

That's hard for people like us to really accept. On one hand we get it, but the radical implications of God's law are offensive to us. Deep down, we think that the Christian life is all about working to get to a place where we are meeting God's demands.

We surmise that if we can at least show God that we've made a little progress towards that end, surely He'll love and accept us. Bur God's law isn't given to us as a blueprint for living the holy life. His law is given to show us who we are NOT!

And yet, we struggle to come to grips with how truly bad we are. We hear the message of God's radical grace for broken and messed up sinners and we think we don't need it as much as the REAL sinners do. We look at our lives and see ourselves as not all that bad. We just need a little help from God. Now those REALLY bad people, they need the kind of radical grace we're talking about here!

Today, I pray that we would allow the reality of God's Law – His unwavering expectations – to slay us. Because when we see how truly unrighteous we are, we are ready to acknowledge that the Gospel is our only hope.

And still, so many of us read these words like they are marching orders given to us by Jesus. A plan for remaining in God's good graces. They become something we strive to attain, believing that if we don't, God will reject us.

The problem with that is this: When we see these words as a standard for Christian living, we are confronted with the reality that we don't even come close to meeting God's expectation of us. And where does that leave us? Hopeless…

But because we who are great sinners have a great Savior, we have been set free from the burden of the Law. We are clothed in the righteousness of Jesus who traded places with us. Our burden has been lifted FOREVER! We who couldn't "get it done" rest in the finished work of Jesus who "GOT it done!"

Let that good news rock your world today!

a prayer for today

God, you are patient, loving, gracious and merciful. I am selfish, brash and fully capable of being insensitive. But you lovingly accept me, not because I have potential to be better, but because of Jesus and His work on the Cross. Thank you for the forgiveness that I don't deserve. Lord, you amaze me. You know me and still you love me. Mind-blowing...

6
"Let's NOT Make A Deal!"

If you look at the music that I have stored on my iPhone you will see that my tastes run the gamut. Some of the songs you'll find will make me look like a fairly cultured music lover – maybe even "cool". However, if you scroll through my list of songs you will find several GUILTY PLEASURE tunes. Hanson, Dolly Parton, Neil Diamond, Rick Springfield, The "Frozen" Soundtrack, and yes – Backstreet Boys. I am a closet Backstreet fan and I stand unashamed!!!

One of their cheesiest – and still a favorite of mine – is a song called, "As Long As You Love Me". You're probably singing it right now. The chorus goes like this:

> *I don't care who you are,*
> *Where you're from,*
> *What you did –*
> *As long as you love me!*

I heard this song one day as I was in the parent-pickup line at school and my first thought was, "This song reminds me of Jesus!" Seriously, it paints a picture of love and acceptance and it even sounds unconditional. But there's that darn last line, "AS LONG AS YOU LOVE ME."

You and I may find ourselves tempted to try to make a deal with God. We trade him our love and allegiance for His grace and mercy.

We bring our devotion and list of promises and He gives us His acceptance. We do our part and He does His part. We meet Him somewhere in the middle and we strike a deal to buy our pardon from sin and, as the old hymn says, "a peace that endureth…"

But come on, there's a part of us that wants to bring something to the mix so that we can feel less like beggars. No one wants to appear desperate and pathetic. Even if we bring just a little to the deal, we can feel better about ourselves. It makes us feel like we're really not THAT bad. But, I contend that in order for the Gospel to be really good news for us, we have to get to that place where we realize how broken and lost we are. Otherwise, we're basically good people trying to get better.

Jen Pollock Michel gets it, you see:

> *"Even the most morally upright person, Christian or non-Christian, falls short of God's glory. In fact, the gospel exposes the depths of my depravity—that of all the pedophiles and pornographers, drunks and derelicts, I am chief sinner among them. And maybe this is the biggest difference between the prostitute and me: not that I outperform her in virtue, but that I outrank her—by virtue of gospel self-awareness—in vice. The gospel doesn't make me better. But it does make me eager to admit my debts and deficits, grateful to receive God's good gifts from whomever's hand they come."* [1]

The Bible describes you and me in the same way Jesus saw the crowds he encountered.

"When he saw the crowds, he had compassion for them, because they were harassed and helpless, like sheep without a shepherd." Matthew 9:36 NLT

Jesus doesn't look at us and see people who are ready to make a deal to earn His favor.

With the eyes of compassion, He sees broken and messed up people who are weary and worn out. He sees desperate sinners with nothing to bring to the table except the sin that made His death necessary. And He asks nothing of us, except that we believe! And the faith that it takes to believe? He gives that to us, too!! We are the helpless receivers and He gives grace, mercy, forgiveness, peace and so much more. None of it comes as a result of any promises we've made. He loves us even knowing that we will fail to love Him back! It really IS one-way love!!

His work on the Cross was not HIS part of the deal to secure our salvation. It is ALL the work necessary to bring us to a place where we are at true peace with God. No strings and no conditions. He won't ever change His mind about you. Even when you take His love for granted and wander down the ugly corridors of life, He will not cast you aside for not holding up your end of the deal. He will pursue you with His love and He will speak over you these words: "My child, you are loved, forgiven and free!"

J.D. Greear says that we are foolish to think we can make deals with God, meeting Him halfway:

"The problem with cutting deals with God is the assumption that we have something he wants. We don't. Think about how foolish our negotiations must sound to God. 'God, how about some extra prayers? How about some church attendance? What if I memorized some more Bible verses?' As if God is up in heaven rubbing his hands, saying, 'Wait, really? You'll go to church more? Now that's an offer I can't refuse! How lucky am I!' We don't have anything that can put God in our debt. There isn't anything we have that he looks at longingly, just waiting for us to offer it to him because he lacks it. We're talking about the Creator of the universe here. What could we possibly offer him that would force his hand?" [2]

It really doesn't matter who you are, where you're from, what you did…BECAUSE HE LOVES YOU! And yes, we who are the receivers of this great gift of Christ's finished work are invited to love Him back. But ours is simply a response. It's not our contribution. Live in the freedom that this great truth provides you today. And if you find yourself loving Him – remember, it's because He loved you first.

a prayer for today

God, you are all I need. I know that. So why do I reach for so many things that are less than you to fulfill me? And when I do, why do you not just give up on me?? I'm so unfaithful to you, despite all that I know about your love for me. Help me to rest in that love today. And when I'm tempted to look elsewhere for love that never satisfies, pull me back to that resting place and remind me of your faithfulness to me. May your love move me to serve you today, Lord. Thanks…

7
We Are Josh Duggar!

Josh Duggar was found out! As a member of TV's The Duggar Family, Josh was seen as an example of purity and virtue. Along with his brothers and sisters, Josh Duggar was part of America's clean-cut family. He was married with children. Josh was hired to represent the Family Research Council, an organization that champions family values. He was on top of the world! He was, but no longer.

Imagine the horror his family felt when it was made public that Josh Duggar had an account with Ashley Madison, a website that helps interested men and women engage in extra-marital affairs. He engaged in behavior that paints a much uglier picture of him than anyone could have ever imagined, including his family. Josh was exposed for the man that he really was. Maybe you're like me and there's at least a part of you that says, "Good! They caught him, that hypocrite."

But Josh Duggar does not stand alone in his guilt. My heart breaks for him because I'm right there with him...

I've been found out, you see. Exposed by God for the fraud that I am. I may have fooled the people around me, but all has been discovered. Everything that I thought I could keep in the dark has been brought out into the light. The hypocrisy of my life is real and true. Now, I didn't engage in the same behaviors that Josh Duggar got caught up in, but my guilt is just the same in God's eyes.

God has exposed all my junk. I am guilty of so many things. I won't get into all the particulars, but my sin would cause you to gasp, at the very least. Almighty God has seen the depths of my darkness and has called me out on all of it - even the sin I wasn't aware of.

BUT, God, who should reject me and cast me aside has done the unthinkable. He sacrificed another in my place. His own Son was given for me. He lived the life that I should live and He died the death that I deserved. Jesus canceled my debt and my account is now marked PAID IN FULL. He looked at His Son on the Cross, saw my sin, and said, "To Hell with you!" Those words were meant for me, but Jesus said, "They're mine..."

Like the old hymn says, "And when I think that God His son, not sparing, sent Him to die, I scarce can take it in. That on the Cross, my burden gladly bearing...He bled and died to take away my sin."

I don't get it. But I so gladly receive it! Paid in full. Totally loved and unconditionally accepted by God. Given new life in Him. His child forever.

Phillip Yancey describes grace this way:

> *"Grace means there is nothing we can do to make God love us more—no amount of spiritual calisthenics and renunciations, no*

amount of knowledge gained from seminaries and divinity schools, no amount of crusading on behalf of righteous causes. And grace means there is nothing we can do to make God love us less —no amount of racism or pride or pornography or adultery or even murder. Grace means that God already loves us as much as an infinite God can possibly love." [1]

What about you? Has the reality of your brokenness hit home? When you think about the ugly parts of your life, do you cringe? Do you want to hide in shame? Well, the good news is this: Jesus is all you need. His covering of your sin is total. And if you believe in Him, your status is changed! Guilty no more. Forgiven and free FOREVER! And there is no condition that you must meet first. God does not ask that you clean up your messy life before you can come to Him.

Here's my reality: If all of my thoughts were to appear on the CNN ticker that runs across the screen at the bottom, my family would

leave me, my church would kick me out, I'd lose my career, and I'd be friendless. I really am that broken. But it's my brokenness that makes me run to the One whom accepts messy people like me. I guess that in some ways, my brokenness is my ugly little friend.

Matt Chandler says that we as believers are identified this way:

"The marker of those who understand the gospel of Jesus Christ is that, when they stumble and fall, when they screw up, they run to God and not from him, because they clearly understand that their acceptance before God is not predicated upon their behavior

but on the righteous life of Jesus Christ and his sacrificial death." [2]

Your debt has been paid and because of Jesus' finished work on your behalf, God looks at you as though you had never ever sinned. You are fully loved and fully accepted by God! You owe nothing and you get everything, my friend. You've been given the best gift anyone has ever received and you got it for free!!!

I wonder how that news will change the way you look at the world today…

a prayer for today

God, I need you today BIGTIME. It's so easy to see the stuff in other people's lives and get really judgey. I don't want to acknowledge how truly messed up I am. But you see the depth of my mess and you choose to love and accept me while I am broken. You call me your child even though I am a rebel and take your love for granted. Make me grateful today, Lord…

8
The Sin We Can't Forget...

Years ago I sat with my friend, Matthew West, who shared an amazing story with me. Matthew is a Christian artist whose music has touched millions around the world. There is probably a radio station playing one of his songs this very second.

Early in his career he was invited to play and sing at a maximum security prison in Tennessee. That day, he sang for rapists, thieves, murderers and molesters. While I'm sure some of them knew his music, this was an opportunity for Matthew to sing for men who were likely strangers to his songs.

After performing an acoustic concert for these men, he was asked to sing a bit more, but not for the general population inmates. The prison officials asked him to sing to the men who were in solitary confinement. In movies and TV shows, these men lived in a part of the prison called "The Hole".

> "When I got there, I was scared. I couldn't see any of these men and that was really intimidating. I stood in the center of the hallway with my guitar and was invited to sing. But I was so scared that I couldn't remember the words to any of my songs! It

really freaked me out. Then I started singing the only words I could remember in that moment":

*"There is no guilt here, there is no shame;
There's nothing left now, there's only grace."*

What a truly powerful moment! Can you imagine what went through the minds of the men listening?

He sang those sweet words to men who were the guiltiest of the guilty. These were the worst offenders in that prison. Society's most awful human beings. He sang about God's grace to THEM!

The reality is that you and I are guilty as charged. Our sin has so sickened God that it deserves harsh condemnation from Him. But Jesus took full and final responsibility for our sin and has removed our guilt and shame. We who deserved judgment have been given grace upon grace. Matthew West's words wash over us and declare that God who is rich in mercy has chosen to forgive us. We are free!!

But still, it's hard for us to accept grace like this. Some who read these words struggle because they are convinced that God couldn't possibly forgive them for the bad choices they've made. I know a girl who refuses to believe that God could forgive her because of the multiple pregnancies that she's terminated.

Still others don't think they're that bad and wonder why they actually need this radical grace we're talking about. They look at their lives and think, "OK, I've sinned like everybody else, but I'm at least trying to be a good person. I mean, it's not like I'm a murderer!"

Each of us needs the forgiveness that Jesus offers. He pours grace into the lives of broken people who realize that their sin-sickness made the Cross necessary. And God promises us that "there is now NO condemnation for those who are in Christ Jesus!"

My life changed years ago when I experienced a "grace awakening".

It was as though I was given a new set of glasses to look at my life through. Gospel lenses blew up everything I believed about God and me. And now I live my life secure in His promises, not mine.

Today, I pray that this good news will overwhelm you in the very best way! I pray that you will be so amazed by the grace you've been given that you'll respond by loving him back. He promises to never cast you aside even if you fail and fall spectacularly today.

And still, you and I will struggle to believe that the radicality of this news is really true! But for those of us who are trusting in Christ's finished work, we will never EVER experience the condemnation of God. Not ever. Jesus has made things right between God and us now and for eternity. And we can't screw this up!! God is no longer our accuser! The Bible says that He who knew no sin BECAME sin for us, so that we might become the righteousness of God! You can come out of the shadows with your ugly secrets without fear of ever being held responsible for them, not ever. I can stand here and say, "I'm a drunk, but Jesus loves me!" And He's giving me the strength to say no to alcohol one day at a time. You can come, too, with your stuff knowing that your standing with God has nothing to do with your ability to manage your struggles. It's all on Him! Jesus has taken full and final responsibility for all of it!

The accuser will call to mind the sins we can't shake. We'll be tempted to try to pay for them ourselves by doing something for God or promising something to God. He invites us to trust in His grace.

There's only grace now…there's only grace.

a prayer for today

God, it's so easy to believe the lie that you are watching me like some cosmic sheriff, waiting for me to screw up. No grace. No mercy. Just judgment. And I deserve all of it. I'm that messed up. But today, Lord, remind me of the truth - the truth of the Gospel that declares that I am forgiven and free because of Christ's work on my behalf. Help me to rest in His work and walk in that freedom today. Thank you for loving this wayward child…

9
A Change Of Identity

In my life I have failed. I have failed huge, in fact. I have experienced relational failures, professional failures and spiritual failures. Some might say that I'm prone to fail. I've given them plenty of reason to believe that.

In 1998, I took a break from my radio career and became the Dean of Students/Campus Pastor at a Christian boarding school in Minnesota. I walked into that job with lots of enthusiasm, passion and vision. I had been a youth pastor for a dozen years early in my adult life so I was pretty sure I could handle this.

After two years in that job I was fired. Frankly, I deserved to be fired. I was terrible at that job. I call my time there "my brief but unhappy career in education"! And while I tried to hold my head up high as we loaded up the truck to head out of town, I was hurting terribly. I had failed. My wife was married to a failure. My son had a failure for a dad.

For six months I couldn't find a job. Oh, and during that time we found out that we were going to have another child. We had no health insurance. I had no idea how we would pay for Larisa to go to the doctor for all of her prenatal visits. One day I made a really hard telephone call to the State of Minnesota to see if we could qualify for welfare medical insurance or something like that. They said yes.

At the end of the call I set down the phone and immediately threw up. I was a failure and no one could tell me otherwise.

After being unemployed for half a year, I got a job in radio once again and was able to resume my career. And even though we were once again in a good place financially, the feelings of inadequacy followed me. I was pretty sure that my failure in Minnesota left a stink on me that everyone could smell. I was a failure and nothing was going to change that. The depression that resulted left me wanting to pull the covers over my head and just stay in bed. I was broken…

This struggle continued for years even though I did my best to put on a happy face. I tried to self-medicate to no avail. In my mind, I was defined by my failures.

But things changed for me when I read a book by Tullian Tchividjian – Jesus + Nothing = Everything. In the pages of this book I read the truth that because the Gospel is true, my identity was now anchored in who God says I am. And he calls me His dearly-loved child. He calls me "Son". And because I'm clothed in the perfect righteousness of Jesus, God is pleased with me! He loves me AND he likes me!!

It took months of soaking in the Gospel but slowly I began to believe that what He said in His word was really true. I started to embrace the idea that I was no longer defined by failure. Jesus had paved the way for me to live a new life with a new identity – an identity that was given to me by God.

I was born to a single mother who raised me alone those first months of my life. When I was 1 ½, she met Ed and married him. Eighteen months later, he adopted me as his son. The old birth certificate was thrown away forever and I was given a new one bearing my father's name. I had been given a new identity!

Can you imagine if I insisted on carrying on with my old name? Legally, I couldn't because I no longer bore that name. That old identity was gone.

Bart Millard, lead singer of MercyMe, underwent an "identity crisis" years ago and after allowing the rich Gospel to take root in His heart, looks at his life and the lives of those around him differently:

> *"It's a shame to meet people who refuse to respond to the message of the cross, but it's just as tragic to meet people who claim to know Jesus but still feel like they are in bondage. From the moment you receive Christ, you are a brand-new creation. When your identity is found in Christ, there is freedom. For all past, present and future sins, Christ already says redeemed. It's the simplicity of the gospel and who you are in Christ—realizing why you can show grace to other people because grace has been shown to you."* [1]

Today, you will be tempted to believe that you, too, are defined by your failures, mistakes, bad choices and rebellion. If you are trusting in Christ by faith, you are a new creation. The old really has passed away and all things are new. And your identity has changed, too. He calls you His dearly-loved child. Believe it! It's true!! And there's nothing you can do to mess this up!!

Walk in freedom today, friend. You are loved…

a prayer for today

God, I need you to remind me of your love for me today. I am so prone to fail and fall - thanks for your promise to never get tired of me. Thanks for not abandoning me in frustration when I deny you and rebel against you. Please keep calling my name and then, Lord, help me to hear your voice. I need you today more than I even know...

10

"I Could Never Believe In A God Who Could Forgive Someone Like Me..."

In the movie, "Rachel Getting Married", Anne Hathaway plays Kym, who is released from rehab for a few days so she can attend her sister's wedding. She is an alcoholic who is getting better and has been sober for several months. Upon arrival at her family's Connecticut home, the atmosphere is obviously strained as her family struggles to deal with the reality of Kym's past AND her present. Her sister resents the fact that Kym's addiction seems to be drawing attention away from the wedding.

In one powerful scene, we discover the reason for the family's strain. Kym tells her story at a Narcotics Anonymous meeting. As a teenager, Kym was responsible for the death of her young brother Ethan, who was left in her care one day; driving home from a nearby park, an intoxicated Kym lost control of the car, driving over a bridge and into a lake, where her brother drowned. Kym and the whole family apparently never recovered from the shock.

In a group therapy session, Kym says something to the others that made me rewind the movie and watch it again 2 or 3 times.

She looks at her fellow addicts and says, **"I could never believe in a God who could forgive someone like me."**

Her family members condemned her for her actions. She condemned herself for the death of her little brother. And frankly, she deserved it! She was supposed to care for him and because she was drunk, he died and it was her fault. She was guilty and her whole world knew it. GOD knew it…

Maybe you know the kind of guilt and shame that Kym felt.

I've known dozens of women who have had abortions – many of them multiple abortions. I have heard them talk of the incredible shame that followed them for years. I know men who have chosen extramarital affairs over their wives and children. The guilt doesn't ever go away, not really.

But God who is so merciful looks at broken sinners like you and me and offers us total and unconditional forgiveness and acceptance. But not until justice has been satisfied. Not until payment has been exacted for our sin. Yes, someone had to be held responsible for our rebellion.

My friend Chad Bird wrote a powerful blog that I read a few months ago about a woman who had terminated a pregnancy. In it, he wrote powerful words about Jesus and the responsibility He took for our sin:

> *"Imagine Jesus saying, 'I will become the one who had the abortion. I will transfer the guilt and regret and heartache she feels onto myself. I will make the voice that accuses her, direct His accusation against me. Once and for all, dear Father, I will become the ocean into which every river of wrong empties itself.*

> No sinner will be left in the world except me. I will be everyone. The guilt, the punishment, the anger, the judgment will all be mine and mine alone. Yes, Father, I will take care of your daughter's abortion. And once I have, we will not speak of it again. We will not remember it again. It will cease to exist.'" [1]

My heart breaks for the "Kyms" of this world who are convinced that God could never forgive what they've done.

They don't feel worthy of grace and mercy because they messed up TOO MUCH. Their offense is TOO GREAT. Is that you? Is that someone close to you?

Please hear the good news today: Jesus took full and final responsibility for your sin and mine! Forever! And he'll never look at you with buyer's remorse. He'll never ever change His mind about you! He won't grow tired of your flakiness as His follower and He will pour His love into your life. Grace upon grace for broken people like us!! The Gospel – it's true…

And as we live and grow as Christians, Jared Wilson says that our dependence on Him because of our unworthiness never wanes:

> *"We walk through victories, successions of freedoms, but my experience has been that the further into Christ's righteousness I press, the more of my own unworthiness I see, not the less. And even as the Spirit bears more and more fruit in my life, even as I learn to trust more and more, when I do finally cross that heavenly finish line, there will nevertheless still be sins unrepented, especially among the sins I don't even remember or don't even see. And I will pull my sorry self across that line, some stupid sin still entangled around my ankle, and I will look up to see Christ the Judge*

standing over me, looking down, considering my pitiful soul. And do you know what he will say? 'Well done.'" [2]

It can be terrifying to shine a spotlight on our sin. It hurts a lot to realize how messed up we are. In AA we are challenged to do a fearless and thorough moral inventory of our lives. Ouch! Then we are directed to be honest about all of it, even admitting it to another person. Double ouch! But the sweet news of the Gospel declares that if we are in Christ, though we be wretched, we are the righteousness of God. We've been cleansed and made pure by Jesus' blood.

How will this reality change the way you approach today? You can either walk in the freedom that the Gospel provides or you can live with that awful weight of unworthiness. Jesus has made you worthy! There is nothing more to be done. The pressure to perform is now off! You can rest in His love and allow it to transform your life.

a prayer for today

God, it's so easy to look at my circumstances and think that you don't really care about me. In your Word, you promise to never leave me. Help me to trust in that today. And, Lord, help me to believe once again that your grace is enough. When, in my weakness, I doubt your love and acceptance, please remind me that my identity is not anchored in anything that I do or don't do. My standing has everything to do with Jesus' finished work on the Cross. Remind me that I am a RECEIVER! Help me to live out of that truth today.

11
Are You Getting It Done?

We live in a world that says to us, "Get it done!" Our success in life is tied directly to our performance.

Think about it – if you work for a company, you likely have a regular "Performance Evaluation". You sit down with your supervisor and he or she answers the question: Are you getting it done? Maybe there is a rating system based on your job description or maybe it's simply a conversation. But the ramifications of this process are pretty huge.

If you're "getting it done", it can mean a salary increase or a promotion. If you're not, it can result in probation, demotion, or maybe even termination. I know people who dread this process because it leaves them tied up in knots. The stress can leave us weary and worn out.

And our kids understand the whole "get it done" thing, too. At school, you get what you earn. If you study adequately for tests and keep up with assignments you get good grades. If you don't work hard to achieve, you likely get bad grades. And if your grades aren't good enough your future could be at stake. I know high schoolers who take the SAT and the ACT three or four times in hopes of earning a high enough score to get into a really good college. And once they get to college, a less-than-stellar GPA could affect a student's job prospects.

We live under a banner that says, "GET IT DONE…OR ELSE!"

The problem with that banner comes when we apply it to our spiritual lives.

The Bible diagnoses us as falling ridiculously short of meeting God's expectations. The Law says to us, "Get it done"! And we just aren't getting it done. We read in Romans 3:23: **"For all have sinned and fall short of God's glory."** No one is getting it done. In Scripture, our best works are compared to filthy rags!

And for those of us who look to find our identity in our accomplishments, this comes as especially bad news. We can't do enough, change enough, improve enough or BE enough to satisfy God's demands.

So Jesus came to live the life we should have lived and to die the death we deserve.

For a long time, I looked at this good news as something of a loan. A temporary fix for my sin. It was like Jesus' death and resurrection bought me some time to get my life right.

Back in the day, appliance and electronics stores offered something to consumers called 90 Days – Same As Cash. You got the TV for free (sort of) for 90 days, but after that you had to start paying for it. Lots of us got sucked into buying a big-ticket item and feeling like we were getting it for free…for three months. Then we had to start paying what we owed.

I lived my life like Jesus died to give me some time to change my behavior, start reading my Bible, and start doing "Christian things"!

But if I didn't use that time to get right with God, He would surely take away the very salvation that I was told I had gotten for free. As a result, I went forward every time there was an altar call. I "rededicated my life to Jesus" dozens of time BECAUSE I WAS AFRAID! Maybe you lived the same thing...

If you are still thinking that grace is just for the beginning of your Christian life, listen to the words of Benjamin Warfield:

> *"There is nothing in us or done by us, at any stage of our earthly development, because of which we are acceptable to God. We must always be accepted for Christ's sake, or we cannot ever be accepted at all. This is not true of us only when we believe. It is just as true after we have believed. It will continue to be true as long as we live. Our need of Christ does not cease with our believing; nor does the nature of our relation to Him or to God through Him ever alter, no matter what our attainments in Christian graces or our achievements in behavior may be. It is always on His "blood and righteousness" alone that we can rest."* [1]

Thankfully, I am learning to get off the terrible treadmill of performance! I was never going to "get it done" so Jesus got it done for me. Once and for all! His perfect performance is now credited to each person who believes. We now live under a new banner: "IT IS FINISHED"!

Could it really be true? Really?

Yes, the Gospel declares that we have been made fully "right" with God. No fear of disappointing Him ever again! We are free to love and serve Him because we GET TO.

Now, is there work to be done? Certainly. I'm in fulltime ministry, so of course there is something for me to do. However, our "work" isn't done to secure or maintain His love and acceptance. We serve Him because we have been fully-loved and fully-accepted. He calls us His sons and daughters!

I pray that this reality will change the way you look at your life today. You and I can't get it done! So we rest in the finished work of Jesus. Rest today, knowing that all the work has been done. He loves you that much.

a prayer for today

Lord, it will be so tempting to believe the lie that somehow I have to do certain things or be a certain way in order for you to be pleased with me. Thanks for the truth of your Word which reminds me that my standing with you has nothing to do with how I perform for you today. It has everything to do with Jesus and His work on my behalf. God, help me to soak in that truth. And may it bring such sweet relief that I will respond to your love by serving you with my life...

12

Just Tell Me What I Have To Do!

And behold, a lawyer stood up to put him to the test, saying, "Teacher, what shall I do to inherit eternal life?" He said to him, "What is written in the Law? How do you read it?" And he answered, "You shall love the Lord your God with all your heart and with all your soul and with all your strength and with all your mind, and your neighbor as yourself." And he said to him, "You have answered correctly; do this, and you will live. Luke 10: 25-28 NLT

I find it interesting that any time a person came to Jesus and asked, "What do I have to do in order to have eternal life?", He just flat-out told them! He pointed to the Law and said, "THIS is what you have to do!"

Now I've heard lots of pastors preach from this text and many of them boil it down to a call to Christians to simply LOVE GOD, and LOVE PEOPLE. I don't think for a minute that this particular text is meant to prescribe the Christian life...at least not in the context of this conversation between Jesus and the lawyer.

The lawyer asks Jesus, "What do I have to do in order to have eternal life?" Jesus says, "Well, if you want to know what to DO, here it is: Love the Lord your God **with all your heart, soul, mind and strength!**

And then He added, "And **love your neighbor as much as you love yourself!**"

Don't be confused into thinking that Jesus was giving this lawyer a plan for salvation. He spoke these words to crush the man. You see, that's what the Law does. It crushes us! It points to a standard that I've never been close to maintaining – not perfectly. And here's the reality, the Law doesn't demand perfection simply in our actions. The Law requires purity of heart and motives.

The truth is this, at least for me: I haven't loved God with all my heart, soul, mind and strength for five total minutes in my life! No, I haven't!! Even my best works are tainted by my sin.

And have I loved my neighbor as much as I love myself? Never! I mean, hey, I'm a nice guy and I try to be good to others, but I have never for a second loved you as much as I love me and mine. If I did, I would choose to give to a family in need instead of treating myself to the latest iPhone. If I loved my neighbor as much as I love myself, I'd take the money that we are planning to spend on that awesome vacation and give it to someone who can't afford to keep their electricity on because of a job loss.

No, the Law wasn't spoken by Jesus in hopes that the lawyer would do what needed doing. He spoke the Law to slay the man. There was no way that this man nor any other man could keep the Law.

That's why there HAD to be a Cross!

Jesus, the only Law KEEPER died to save Law BREAKERS who didn't stand a chance without His intervention. He lived the perfect life that was required of us, and then died the death that was deserved by us.

And then Jesus pointed to a new work required by God:

"Then they said to Him, 'What must we do to be doing the works of God?" Jesus answered them, 'This is the work of God, that you believe in whom He has sent." John 6:28-29 NLT

He made it simple enough that a thief hanging on a Cross next to Jesus could simply say, "Remember me...", and He was promised eternal life.

Robert Capon describes grace this way:

> *"Salvation is not some felicitous state to which we can lift ourselves by our own bootstraps after the contemplation of sufficiently good examples. It is an utterly new creation into which we are brought by our death in Jesus' death and our resurrection in his. It comes not out of our own best efforts, however well-inspired or successfully pursued, but out of the shipwreck of all human efforts whatsoever."* [1]

If you believe in Him you have been made right with Him! No longer do we need to live in fear again. We who were lost have been found! We who were spiritually blind have been given our sight! He loves us and has already judged Jesus in our place. We who are weary and worn out because we thought there was a code we must abide by or else – we are free to rest in the good news of what He's done without wondering how He feels about us. He loves us!

Go live today from THAT place!

a prayer for today

God, as much as I know you forgive me and love me, I find it so easy to focus on those regrets that I have. I have hurt others in profound ways and I deserve the condemnation of those who have been on the receiving end of my sin. I cringe when I play back those tapes. This is precisely why I need you to remind me of who I am because of what Jesus has done. Help me, Lord, to walk in the newness of life. And as you do this work in me, I pray that I'll be obedient to leave those failures and regrets in the past. May your love for me be so overwhelming that I'll experience the joy of a man whose sins are forgiven. Thank you, God, for your love and acceptance.

13
The Tandem Jumper I Need To Be...

I am afraid of heights. If I have to climb a ladder to change the battery in the smoke detector, I get a bit freaked out. Years ago, I went bungee jumping off a crane at Ft. Myers Beach in Florida but I was drunk. Being up high? Not my thing.

I have been invited several times to go skydiving. I have politely refused each invitation. Maybe it's because I've read too many stories about chutes that wouldn't open, but just thinking about jumping out of a plane makes my blood pressure go up and a bit of sweat form on my brow.

But my friends say stuff like, "But it's really not that bad because the first time you jump, you always go TANDEM!" Hmmm...tandem. This is where you are tethered to an experienced jumper who does all the work. He pulls the cord at exactly the right time – you just fall and enjoy. You are led, guided and protected by a qualified person with dozens and maybe even hundreds of jumps to his credit.

The idea of going tandem removes not one bit of the fear from me, so I won't be adding skydiving to my bucket list.

The thing about parachuting is that once you've gotten enough training and experience, you can go it alone. No longer do you need to be tethered to a more seasoned jumper. No longer do you need the security of your tandem leader (if that's what he's called). You've gotten to a point where you don't need as much help!

Spiritually, we get really fouled up when we look at our lives this way.

I think that there's a mentality in the church that gives believers the impression that when we first come to faith, we need a lot of Jesus. We are desperate for His love, His acceptance and His guidance. We are told to tether ourselves to Him and walk in the newness of life. Sort of in the same way that a newborn needs mommy close by at all times.

But then as we grow in our faith – as we become more MATURE as believers – we seem to live like we need less and less Jesus in our lives. We are able to stand strong on our own with the hope that Jesus isn't too far away (just in case we find ourselves drowning in quicksand)! We think that as we get stronger, our need for Him is less than it once was.

Now maybe we don't consciously say this, but many of us live like the parachuter who longs to be able to jump alone and not need to be tethered to someone stronger. We don't like to be weak and needy. I mean, that's a sign of immaturity, right?

And we put so much stock in our changed lives. Our testimony of better living and increasingly moral behavior becomes the thing we hang our hat on.

Worship Pastor Zac Hicks says this:

> *"The root of faith is not me or my transformed life; it is Christ and His life and death. Christianity does not begin with the good news of my life changed, but Christ's life exchanged!"* [1]

Hebrews 11 is filled with the names of people who learned (sometimes the hard way) that they were broken sinners who desperately needed to be tethered to a faithful and compassionate God who would work in and through them – and often times, despite themselves.

We who have the benefit of living on this side of the Cross are just as broken and just as sinful. And Jesus our Savior tethers HIMSELF to US!

He promises to be all we need. His finished work on the Cross saves us and now we walk in freedom! And it isn't our tethering ourselves to Him that gives us hope each day. It's the truth that Jesus is holding on to us that matters. His grip is secure. His promise to hold tight won't ever change.

Matt Smethurst reminds us that our standing with God has everything to do with our living in tandem:

> *"In the world, status is tethered to performance. It's the same in the gospel. The difference, however, is that our status as believers is not tethered to our performance, but Christ's. Only the gospel can offer the resources to combat our pride, expose our emptiness, and flood our hearts with peace."* [2]

You will be tempted to live your life on your own, relying on whatever strength you can muster up. You might believe the lie that your sin is so great that you better get to work making up for all your failures and mistakes. You'll be told to suck it up and "never let 'em see you sweat"! But there is a much better way.

Today, be a tandem jumper! He's got you. He really does. And tomorrow, you'll need Him as much as you do today. Is that weakness? Maybe. But I'll take His strength any day...

a prayer for today

Lord, I come to you believing that you are real and that you love me. Your grace and mercy are given to me despite the fact that I tend to take all of it for granted. Remind me that I am a desperate sinner who doesn't meet your holy expectations. And please, Lord, don't let me forget the wideness of your mercies. May the reality of your radical love make me glad today. Fill me with that love and help me to love those around me - especially the ones I'd rather ignore. Thanks, God...

14

Fathers And Their Children

It's so interesting: I've never met a dad who doesn't love his kids. Never! Even the guys I've visited with in prison, who've done unspeakable things, still love their kids. And THEIR parents still love THEM!

But I've met a lot of fathers over the years who don't seem to like their kids very much. These dads are generally not ever pleased with their children. They seem to take little joy in being their kids' father. Time spent with their children is difficult and uninteresting to them.

Years ago I heard from a teenage girl who shared her honest feelings about her father:

> *"I don't expect my dad to understand my world, but I do want my dad to TRY to understand ME! He seems disappointed in everything I say and do. My grades are good, but not good enough. I don't have the right friends. I don't have goals. I'm not the super-Christian girl that my sister is. I don't do enough around the house. My room is not as perfect as he'd like. Nothing I do is enough!! I just want him to be happy with me – because I'm HIS*

DAUGHTER! I want him to be pleased with me. I want him to like me! But apparently, I'm nothing but a disappointment."

Isaiah prophesied about Jesus: **"Behold my servant whom I uphold, my chosen in whom my soul is well-pleased." Isaiah 42:1 NLT**

God the Father was pleased with His Son Jesus. He is the perfect Son. He never disappoints His Father. His character is flawless and His motives are always pure.

We love to sing Chris Tomlin's "Good, Good Father" and while the chorus is a beautiful declaration of who God is and who we are, there is a line we can't miss before we get to the chorus:

"And you tell me that you're PLEASED and that I'm never alone..."

What a powerful statement!! He's pleased with us! Despite knowing the depth of our sin-sickness, He says He's pleased with us. He is well-acquainted with our wretchedness and yet He says we are pleasing to Him. How can it be?

You see, Jesus – in whom God was fully pleased - has transferred His standing to us. Our Father now finds His children pleasing. Not because of anything that you and I have done or will do, but because of the finished work of Jesus on our behalf. He delights to show us mercy!

He loves to lavish us with love and grace. His promises are now ours to hold onto. Nothing can ever separate us from His love. He pledges to never leave us nor forsake us.

I am a very flawed dad. Just ask my kids. They have seen me at my worst and most broken. I have had to ask for much forgiveness from them. Because of my years of alcohol abuse, I am left with only a few memories of when they were really little. That hurts to say.

I know I was there during their early years, but I can't remember much. Who does that to their kids? Here God had given me two terrific kids and I became a drunk before their eyes. Now I guess I'm trying to make up for some of that. I tell them all the time now how pleased I am that they are MY kids.

The Gospel is not God's pronouncement that He is excusing our sin - simply giving us a pass. It is His declaration that once and for all sin has been dealt with! Jesus has taken full and final responsibility for all of it! Your Father has provided for you and has done for you what you could never do for yourself!

I'm now learning that it's ok to share some of the dark parts of my life. It's in those places that Jesus meets me with grace and mercy. So often we fear that exposing our brokenness will cause people to run from us. I've actually found the opposite to be true. I hear from so many strugglers like me who say, "I thought I was the only one." The Gospel sounds sweetest to the ones who are desperate for the relief it brings. I'm one of those desperate ones. I come to Him broken and messed up. And He calls me His dearly-loved child.

Whatever you've done and whatever wreckage you've left behind – your Father is waiting to bathe you in forgiveness. He's ready to pour grace and mercy all over you, now and forever.

You don't need to be afraid to face your Father. He knows you and He loves you. He has made full satisfaction for your sin because of Christ's work on your behalf.

Your dad may have been a bust. He may have failed to make you feel valued and appreciated. But your Heavenly Father loves you perfectly and has declared you fully pleasing to Him. And because your dad was imperfect, it might be hard to accept the love of God. By faith, believe that everything the Bible says about you is true! You are fully-loved, fully-accepted and fully-known. And there's nothing you can do to wreck that!!

How will that impact your day today?

a prayer for today

God, I can be so self-absorbed and I live with a "me first" attitude so much of the time. Today I'll be tempted to focus on being good and well-behaved. I'll do this thinking that if I can be better and more improved, you'll love me more and bless me more. Remind me today that I'm truly forgiven and free. And may your radical love for broken guys like me free me to focus on loving those around me. And help me, Lord, to love them genuinely.

15

A Safe Place To Fall...

December 13, 1985 will go down in history as one of the worst nights of my life. I've had many hard days, but this day nearly wrecked me. I was a twenty-year-old Youth Pastor in the Seattle area and a few minutes before midnight I got a phone call that would affect me for life.

Janet was one of my "kids" and earlier that night she was at our youth group Christmas party. I will never forget hearing her voice on the phone late that night: "Jeff, Trish is gone. She was in a terrible accident tonight. Tina died, too, and Elisabeth is hurt badly and she might not make it. Please come to the hospital. We need you here."

Trish was Janet's older sister and Elisabeth was a dear friend. These kids were a big part of our youth group. I drove twenty minutes to the hospital that night. On the way, I passed the accident scene. The car was unrecognizable. I was not in any way prepared for the next several hours.

When I arrived at Providence Hospital I encountered three grieving families. Two of those families were dealing with the death of their daughters. One family watched as their daughter fought for her life.

I had no words. I tried to just be present with them as they worked through the first hours following this tragedy. As each hour passed, the hole in my heart grew. But I tried to be strong.

After nearly six hours at the hospital with those families, I went home. But I couldn't sleep. I felt more heartache than I ever had before. But I tried to be strong.

Over the next several hours, I called more than one hundred kids to tell them that their friend had been killed and that another friend was in a coma. Those calls were so painful to make. I wanted someone else to make them. I wished I could crawl into bed, pull the covers over my head and hide in my pain. But I tried to be strong.

After a day spent making hard phone calls I found myself sitting alone in my apartment wishing that I had a place to go. I got into my car and drove four blocks to Randy and Diane's house. They were a couple that had sort of taken me in during my years in Seattle. Their house was the only place I wanted to be at that moment.

When Randy answered the door, I fell apart, collapsing into his arms. It was the first time I had cried. He held me as I sobbed and sobbed. No lie – tears are falling right now as I write these words. He bore the weight of my pain in that moment standing in the doorway. Diane made me dinner and for an hour or so, they let me fall apart. They spoke no profound words that night. They let me be weak. It was such a great gift.

The next few weeks were hard. I had to be strong, I thought. But my dear friends gave me permission to be a grieving weakling. And because of that, I was able to lead our youth group despite my broken heart. I slowly abandoned the desire to be seen as the strong guy everyone could follow through this dark place. I found comfort in knowing we could all be weak together.

When I was nineteen years old, I was diagnosed with Crohn's Disease. It's a chronic illness that cannot be cured. I'd explain the symptoms for you, but they're not pleasant to experience nor discuss. It has rendered me weaker than I used to be. I wear out easily and sometimes the pain is great. Crohn's is both my nemesis and my friend. You see, I am learning that having a disease that will never go away makes me a bit of a weakling. But it reminds me that God's power is mine.

Ray Ortlund understands the power of weakness in the lives of believers:

> "So Paul saw weakness not as evidence against himself but as the way of power and the wonderful surprises that only God can orchestrate. It is his way for us all. The super-apostles knew nothing of it. All they understood was trying to be impressive, which they were, but that kind of fraudulent power threatened the integrity and the very future of the Corinthian church. Authentic Christianity does not produce a race of supermen who rise above need; the most perfect expression of authentic Christianity in this age is divine power received with the empty hands of human weakness and poverty and pain." [1]

Ortlund was speaking about this verse that might be quite familiar to you:

"But he said to me, 'My grace is sufficient for you, for my power is made perfect in weakness.' Therefore I will boast all the more gladly of my weaknesses, so that the power of Christ may rest upon me." 2 Corinthians 12:9 ESV

Our fears expose our lack of faith. We're afraid because we don't trust God. But He overcomes our fear with His love for us in Christ – a love specifically for those who don't deserve it.

Because the Gospel is true, you and I no longer have to fake strength. We are weak and HE IS STRONG. We can leave our masks in the closet and face the world as weak. It really is ok to be a weakling! Whatever you face today, know that His power is made perfect in our weakness. So be weak. And watch as He becomes your strength. Notice, I didn't say that He would make you strong. The Bible says that He will BE OUR STRENGTH. Collapse into His arms. It's the safest place to be…

a prayer for today

Lord, it's so easy to let the circumstances of my life overwhelm me. Really, God, it's sometimes so hard to just get through the day. I will be tempted today to put on a shiny happy face and hide behind that mask. You know that I want people to think I have it together. May the reality of your grace give me the strength to live honestly and authentically today. And God, please remind me that when I am weak, YOU are strong. Please be my strength today…

16

"This Is My Beloved Son, In Whom I Am Well-Pleased!"

Does the name Graeham Goble ring a bell? Probably not. He was a founding member of Australian super group The Little River Band of the 70's and 80's. He wrote most of their music and amazingly couldn't read a note! With hits in both Australia and America, the band sold more than 30 million records and cemented itself as one of Australia's best bands of all-time.

Goble wrote a song in the late '70's which would become the band's biggest hit. "Reminiscing" was a worldwide smash and became a classic. It continues to be played on radio stations 40 years later. But it's what one great musical icon said about that song that strikes me as huge.

If you walk into Graeham Goble's studio today, you will see these words written on the wall of the entry: "'REMINISCING' DEFINED THE '70's!" – Frank Sinatra

I literally get chills writing those words. Yes, I'm that much a music nerd. I was raised on radio!

What an affirmation! THE Frank Sinatra says that a song YOU wrote defined an entire decade. If I were Graeham Goble, I'd have those words hanging somewhere in my home, studio, car or I'd have them tattooed on my arm. One of the greatest of all-time offering the ultimate compliment – "Your song defined the 1970's!" I'm not sure that I could write another song, ever.

What a blessing pronounced on a song that YOU wrote!

When Jesus was baptized, God spoke powerful words of blessing and affirmation on Him:

"And behold, a voice from heaven said, 'This is my beloved Son, with whom I am well pleased.'" Matthew 3:17 ESV

What a statement from Almighty God about His Son! The ultimate blessing from the One whose affirmation really mattered. It propelled Jesus into His adult ministry. God smiled on His perfect, holy Son and affirmed His role and plan for the redemption of mankind.

Frank Sinatra's affirmation of Graeham Goble's songwriting prowess was a powerful statement, but God's blessing spoken upon His Son was so much more meaningful and impressive. The words came from GOD, not just a musical icon.

So what does this mean for you and me? Sit down because it's huge!

Because the Gospel is true, you and I who believe in Jesus are given the same blessing that He was given. Because we, who are sin-soaked are now called sons and daughters of Almighty God! We have been credited with the righteousness of God in Christ!

God who knows our wretchedness now looks at us and says, "This is my son/daughter _____ in whom I am now well-pleased!! We are loved like we were Jesus himself.

The greatest affirmation and blessing ever given was not given by Frank Sinatra. It has been pronounced by God himself, who declares you and me "beloved children in whom He is well-pleased!" The very blessing spoken to Jesus by His Father is now spoken over us! We bear His name. We are now joint heirs with Jesus himself, and boy does that sound good!

So if this is true, then we have been given the ultimate blessing from God. Jesus has made us pleasing to God, once and for all time! How will the reality of this good news impact the way you live your life today?

Will you live in fear that God is waiting to let you know how disappointed He is in you? Or will you rest in the blessing that Jesus won for you? That sounds like an absurd question, but really – which question defines the Christian life for you right now? For so long, I lived in fear. I desperately wanted to be pleasing to Him, but I thought in my heart of hearts, that he must be upset with me and my lack of progress as a Christian. The Gospel has reoriented me and my thinking. It brings me good news!

The Bible says that we are His redeemed children. That makes me walk a little lighter each day. How bout you? Will it impact the way you approach the circumstances of your life today? Will you look at others from a different perspective because this good news is true? Can His declaration of unconditional love and acceptance transform your life today?

I'm as insecure as anyone and I've struggled to believe that His love and acceptance really were secured for me, now and forever. In my head I know it, but to really believe it in my heart is a different story. I was convinced that my standing with God was ultimately on me. It's why I struggled for so long. But the more I preach the Gospel to myself, the more I am learning to believe this great truth and rest in it. His pronouncement that because of Christ He can now call me His son blows my mind. How can it be? It's true because His Word says it's true!

As Michael Horton says,

> "The Gospel is not wishful thinking. It's not just optimistic or sentimental uplift. It's the announcement of a fact!" [1]

Let the good news of the Gospel wash over you and believe it! Its message is for you!! Jesus loves you, friend…and you can't chase Him away. And if you believe, you are now marked by HIS name!

a prayer for today

God, I will be tempted today to present a version of myself to the world that is fake and false. I want people to see me as strong and secure. You know that I'm not. You know the weakness that I try to hide from everyone and you welcome me, not in spite of it, but because of it! Give me the strength to live authenticity today, Lord…

17

I Am Truly The Worst Man In America!

I remember seeing the headline, as though it were yesterday. A major American newspaper called former Presidential and Vice-presidential candidate John Edwards "The Worst Man In America!"

He was pretty despicable, actually. His devoted wife, who stood by his side throughout his private and political career, had been diagnosed with a recurrence of cancer. This time, it was really serious. America was saddened by the news. Democrats and Republicans offered prayers and support for Elisabeth Edwards, as well as the entire family. She was so very sick.

In the midst of her journey with great sickness, it came out that her husband, Sen. John Edwards, who ran for President and later was on the Democratic ticket as a potential VP, had fathered a child with another woman. The national news reports were divided between her cancer, which was now terminal, and her husband's infidelity. It was the ultimate in bad news.

John was vilified by those on both sides of the political aisle. As his wife lay dying, his sin lived large as America watched like it was a sporting event. Like one newspaper wrote, John Edwards was the worst man in America. At least that was the perception.

What a jerk! What a selfish fool who should have known better!! What a disgraced awful human being.

I found myself joining the public in condemning this man. He was a horrible man!!!

But then, I realized something. I was just as bad as him. I was just as broken as John Edwards. I was just as guilty as he was. At least that's what God says…

The awful reality of Jeff Taylor is that I am sin-soaked. My record is horribly blemished. I'm a liar, a cheat, a fraud and a hypocrite. If my thoughts were displayed on the big screens at church, my family would abandon me, my church would kick me out and I'd be left alone, without a job and without anyone on my team. I am as guilty as John Edwards, you see. And so are you, according to the Bible.

As my friend Jim Griffin reminds me from time to time, the ground is level at the foot of the Cross. We, each of us, stand shoulder to shoulder, guilty as hell! The stench from our wretchedness is awful. And there we stand…100% guilty under God's Law. No one worse than another. This is a really important point, because so many of us think we're not that bad. We deceive ourselves into believing that it's those other people who need the REAL help. We just need a little guidance and encouragement to "keep on keeping on".

The Apostle Paul wrote these transparent words:

"The saying is trustworthy and deserving of full acceptance, that Christ Jesus came into the world to save sinners, of whom I am the foremost." I Timothy 1:15 NLT

I join him in this statement. For I am the worst of sinners. I am John Edwards and more. I've been declared guilty and deserving of death and hell.

BUT GOD, according to Ephesians 2, who is rich in mercy, has made us alive even though we were dead in our sins!!! Because the Gospel is true, He declares us, "NOT GUILTY", now and forever because of Jesus and His finished work on the Cross.

We are now justified fully because of Christ. And when we, by faith, receive Him, we are no longer held accountable for our sin. Instead, we are clothed in the righteousness of Jesus himself!! Free! And even as I write these words, there is a part of me that thinks this is all too good to be true! How could He possibly love me that much? How could He pardon a sinner like me?

Pastor Nick Lannon offers this simple, yet profound explanation of what Jesus' sacrifice was all about:

> *"Jesus took all the self-righteousness of the 'good people' and all the failings of the 'bad people' with Him to the Cross. In Him we are redeemed."* [1]

So, in light of this good news, how will you respond? Do you even believe that it's true for you? Will you allow it to liberate you and give you freedom and confidence as you navigate through this day? You have been declared, "NOT GUILTY!" Let that sink in a bit. Your Heavenly Father knows all of your junk, yet because of Jesus, He promises to never hold it against you! Do you dare believe this to be true?

Or, you can live under the weight of your sin-sickness. You can hope that at the end of time you will have done enough to satisfy Him. You can pray that your good outweighs your bad when God assesses your life. You can hope that you've done enough to secure His acceptance. But the Bible says you haven't and won't. That's why there was a Cross! That's why Jesus came. His life, death and resurrection were all about you and me – wretched sinners with no hope. But the Savior has done all that needed to be done – even for the worst among us. We now have hope! Not in our ability to become better people, but hope in Christ!

a prayer for today

God, you are faithful when I am not. As much as I want to be committed to you, I am reminded in your Word that my standing with you has everything to do with how committed YOU are to me. Sometimes I feel pressured by others to make lots of promises to you. But you know how bad I am at keeping them. Thank you, Lord, for making promises to me that are rock solid and can never be broken. Help me to rest in those promises today. And may your grace motivate me to love you and others more...

18

Yes, Grace...But What About OBEDIENCE?

Because I am something of a Gospel fire hydrant who can't seem to quit talking about grace, I get challenged sometimes by well-intentioned folks who are concerned that all this grace talk will surely lead to laziness and a life with no emphasis on obedience to God's Word. I mean, hey – even in the New Testament there are plenty of "imperatives" and we can't ignore those.

I believe that the letters in the New Testament, written to the various churches, were given to describe in detail what the liberated life looks like. And they are a statement of God's BEST for His children. They aren't given to us so because God is the great cosmic killjoy! They are given to us, as Luther puts it, "to show us how to live."

The problem for a lot of believers is that their pastor preaches the "imperatives" without putting them in the context of the "indicatives". Notice how Paul wrote most of his letters by first stating who we are in Christ because of His finished work. Then in the back half of his letters he would exhort the church to live in a new way – and not SO THAT God would love and accept them, but BECAUSE God loves and accepts those who simply believe.

When the Gospel captivates us, it slowly begins to fuel our obedience to God. We live in response to His love for us. And we grow in our trust that His commands are BEST for us. We do this knowing that even on our best day, our obedience doesn't come close to earning us anything from Him.

Matt Chandler sees obedience as a natural response:

> *"If you are in Christ (and that's a huge sentence), you have done nothing and can do nothing to turn the affection-filled gaze of God away from you. That's stunning, and Paul says that compels him. The work of the gospel, this love of God made manifest in the person and work of Jesus Christ, this love of God that compelled Paul toward obedience, had completely rewired his heart."* [1]

I look at obedience this way:

When I was 45, I decided to get braces because my teeth were crooked and stuck out a little. Eighteen months later, my orthodontist gave me a smile that I was proud to show! On the occasion of my last visit, I was fitted with a plastic retainer and was told to wear it each night. This would keep my teeth straight.

My retainer looked like a mouth guard – like the one I wore playing football in high school. I was supposed to wear it diligently. Um, that never happened. I had no interest in wearing that thing every night while I slept. So I shoved it in a drawer.

A few weeks ago, I noticed that my teeth were moving a bit and I figured that wasn't a good thing. After all, I had spent thousands getting my teeth straightened and I was not going to let things get any worse. So I started wearing my retainer.

No one was pointing a gun to my head. My orthodontist wasn't calling me to find out if I was following the rules.

I just decided that doing what my doctor told me was the very best thing for me and my smile! Larisa, my wife, wouldn't withhold her love if I let me teeth get crooked again. My boss wouldn't fire me if I didn't comply with the wishes of my orthodontist. The cops wouldn't show up at my front door because I was failing to do what I had been told.

I simply reached a place where after 45 years, I had a smile that I was proud of. I wanted it to stay that way.

Wearing the retainer is the best thing for me so I'm listening to my doctor and doing what he says. And my teeth are looking pretty good!

Here's what Ross Lester says about the Gospel's affect on our living:

> *The gospel isn't a declaration that I need to be good, but rather that Christ is already good, and has bestowed that goodness upon those who are no good. We then seek to live differently because of how good he has already shown us he is, rather than in the vain hope of we ourselves being good enough. We must obey, to be sure, but our obedience is as a result of his affection and not in an attempt to earn it.* [2]

I pray that today you will discover the joy of Gospel-fueled obedience. It gets you nothing from God. You already have His full love and acceptance already because of Jesus. Your obedience to Him is simply an acknowledgement that His best for you is what your heart longs for. It's the loving response of a grateful sinner.

Now where did I put that retainer…

a prayer for today

God, I pray that you'd work in me today, that I might reflect your love to others. It's so easy to be self-absorbed, but as you remind me of who I am because of what Jesus has done, may your radical grace do its transforming work in me. And as I soak in your love, help me to share it with those around me.

19
Regarding Henry...

In the movie, "Regarding Henry", Harrison Ford plays ruthless New York lawyer Henry Turner. Henry was smug, self-absorbed, cold-hearted and uncaring. He had a wife whom he was cheating on. He had a daughter with whom he had little relationship. She lived in fear of failing to meet her father's expectations. Henry was a wealthy and professionally-successful jerk.

One night before going to bed, Henry realized that he was out of cigarettes. He got dressed and walked a few blocks to the neighborhood bodega to buy a pack. When he opened the door to enter the store, it was clear that he had walked into the middle of an armed robbery. He looked at the gunman and said, "Come on, man, give me a break" smugly. The robber proceeded to shoot him in the shoulder and then the head.

Henry was rushed to the hospital where he laid in a coma for a week or so. When he woke from the coma, he couldn't speak nor could he control his motor skills. But he was alive! He survived a bullet to the brain.

The next months were filled with speech and physical therapy. Slowly, Henry began to recover his ability to walk, talk, eat and drink. It was a long, slow process but Henry set recovery records.

It was quite amazing. Eventually, Henry completed his long rehabilitation and was poised to begin his life again in the world he once knew.

When Henry went home to live with his wife and daughter, he was obviously different.

The gunshots did damage that he didn't realize until he got back to his world. Many of the things he used to like weren't appealing to him anymore. He went back to his law firm but soon discovered that he didn't really like being a lawyer.

But the real difference in Henry was seen in the way he related to his wife and daughter. Before being shot, he had a wife whom he didn't love anymore. Now he seemed to enjoy every moment he spent with her. The daughter who lived in fear of her father was now becoming her dad's favorite person. They spent lots of time together and had a growing relationship. All of this was simply unimaginable prior to the gunshot.

You see, the bullet that should have killed him became the bullet that CHANGED Henry Turner…

It took a tragic gunshot wound for Henry to experience what no one on Earth could do for him. It was a complete reset for him. He was a completely different man and his life reflected it in every way. He wasn't perfect at all, but that bullet reoriented him.

2 Corinthians 5:17 says, "Therefore, if anyone is in Christ, he is a new creation. The old has passed away, behold, the new has come."

Because the Gospel is true, we now live as new creatures. The Cross doesn't just save us, it reorients us. Like a bullet to the brain it makes us new and different people. You see, when you are in Christ, trusting in His finished work, the Holy Spirit does His job reproducing the character of Christ in you.

The change isn't always dramatic or easy to see from the outside. We are always living with the reality of our sin struggle. And don't forget this: Your ability to live in a new way as a believer garners you no extra favor from God. It doesn't keep you in His good graces. In fact, the change that you experience isn't your work, but rather, it is His work in you!

Does the Gospel mean something for us on a daily basis? Yes. Does it affect the way we live? Yes. But the Gospel does not announce that we are at peace with God as long as we climb up onto the treadmill of performance and keep our "Daddy" happy! Not at all. It gives us everything we need to live FROM our salvation, not in order to get a little more of it. We are free to love and serve Him imperfectly! He won't ever turn us away for not doing it right.

Scotty Smith wrote this sweet Gospel-drenched prayer:

> *"In Christ, you've given us a completely forgiven past, a present standing in grace, and a future of unimaginable wonder. But what really encourages me today is to realize, yet again, that all of this heavenly goodness is guaranteed. You've "sealed the deal" by the Holy Spirit. You've given us the down payment, firstfruits, and*

promise of a future beyond our wildest dreams, imagining, and asking." [1]

Talk about transformation! So today, live knowing that God is at work, changing your heart and changing your mind. For Henry, it took a bullet. For you and me, it took a Cross.

a prayer for today

God, I need you today - for so much. I will be tempted to show you that I am less dependent on you in hopes that you'll reward me for growing beyond my dependence on you. That's just wrong. I come to you as a needy struggler and I will live this day trusting that you won't leave me, because I'm nothing without you, Lord. Forgive me for failing and falling today. And, please, hold me close. Keep me from wandering...

20
I Get By With A Little Help...

If I'm being honest, it concerns me when people point to Jesus as our example for living. They see Him as a role model. Granted, Jesus is the visible expression of the invisible God, and there is much to be gleaned from studying His words and His life. But before we can ever look to Him as an example, we need to see Him as something much more than that.

In the book of Mark we read a powerful story about Jesus. One day, Jesus had been speaking to the crowds, painting a picture of what the Kingdom of God was like. Imagine how worn out anyone would be dealing with crowds of people all day. When all was done, Jesus needed to rest.

"On that day, when evening had come, he said to them, 'Let us go across to the other side.' And leaving the crowd, they took him with them in the boat, just as he was. And other boats were with him. And a great windstorm arose, and the waves were breaking into the boat, so that the boat was already filling. But he was in the stern, asleep on the cushion. And they woke him and said to him, 'Teacher, do you not care that we are perishing?' And he awoke and rebuked the wind and said to the sea, 'Peace! Be still!' And the wind ceased, and there was a great calm. He said to them, 'Why are you so afraid? Have you still no faith?'" Mark 4:35-41 NLT

These were experienced, professional fishermen who had sailed through many storms before, I'm sure. Imagine the panic as they were bailing water as fast as they could to no avail. This was the big one! Their lives were flashing before their eyes. No matter how hard they tried, this collection of men couldn't save themselves. So they woke the sleeping Jesus who was in the stern of the boat.

"Don't you care that we're all going to die here, Jesus!?!"

Jesus climbed to the deck and did the miraculous. He spoke to the wind and the waves telling them, "Peace! Be Still!" And the Bible says that at that moment, the storm died down and the seas were calm.

He didn't do this to demonstrate to his disciples the manner in which they, too, could stop a storm. He did this, I believe, to paint a picture of who He was and what He had come to Earth to accomplish. When the disciples were facing certain death because of a horrific storm, Jesus did for them what they could not do for themselves. He RESCUED them!

The Gospel is simply good news about Jesus who has done for us what we couldn't do for ourselves. While we were lost in sin, facing the certain wrath of God, Jesus left Heaven, became one of us, lived a perfectly righteous life and died in our place. He rescues sinners like you and me and even gifts us with the faith to believe in Him! That was hard for me to wrap my brain around. I thought for most of my life that faith was something that I mustered up. Faith grew because of my hard work living like a good Christian. I lived my life like faith was my gift to God, not His gift to me. It was about me and my effort.

But the Gospel shoots that down! There is nothing more for us to do to secure God's love and acceptance. We receive from Him the very thing that was unattainable. And He gives it freely. There are no strings attached. No prerequisites. No conditions to meet first. It's free! Believe it!!

If the Good News of God's radical grace for broken and messed up people doesn't sound too good to be true, you probably didn't hear the GOOD NEWS! I mean, it flies in the face of what we know and believe about life: You GET based on what you ACHIEVE. The harder you work, the more successful you'll be. Nothing comes to us for free - you have to earn it! But the Gospel blows all that up.

Jesus the Rescuer came to demonstrate the love of God. He didn't come to give us a hand. God's grace comes to you and me based on nothing we do nor have done. It is given freely to people who don't deserve it and will take it for granted! We are at peace with God because of the work of another - Jesus. He has made things right! It says to the broken and messed up rebel in all of us, "I love you and nothing you ever do or don't do can change that."

Now that the rescue work has been done once and for all, we can rest in that truth. Jesus died for all mankind, but for Him it was also personal: He took your name to the Cross. What's it like to know that you are loved THAT MUCH? Yes, the news is good today! Let it relieve you. Know that there is nothing you can do that will invalidate the transaction that took place at Calvary.

You and I need more than a life coach and an example to follow. We need someone to do for us what we can't do for ourselves. That's why He came. He came for you.

Have a sweet day, my friend…

a prayer for today

God, it's so easy to try to do a lot of things that will make me look better in your eyes. I will deceive myself into thinking that somehow my behavior will affect your love and acceptance of me. Lord, help me to recognize this and live FROM your grace and not to EARN a little more from you. And I pray that the good news of your radical love for me will bring relief but will also move me to live in a new way as I respond to your grace…

21
A Picture Of Grace That Might Offend You...

I heard Dr. Steve Brown tell a story about a boy named Justin. I shared it on the radio and people loved it...and some hated it.

Justin was 10 years old and lived in a home that sat on a small cul-de-sac. He was a well-liked kid. He had found out that his neighbors were going to move away and he didn't like that at all. He loved his neighbors and the thought of them leaving broke his heart. He decided to do something about it.

One day, when he was sure no one was looking, he went into the neighbor's house, plugged up all the drains, turned the water on and flooded the house. The damage to that house was huge.

Each evening at the dinner table, his family would talk about how awful this was and together they kept asking the question, "Who would do something like this?" Justin did his best to look innocent. But each night as he lay in bed, Justin agonized over his actions. He begged forgiveness from God. But how could God forgive him for doing such a despicable thing. The guilt and shame he felt only grew.

One day Justin was out playing with his friends in the cul-de-sac when his father called him inside to talk.

"Justin, was it you who flooded the neighbor's house?", Dad asked. Justin denied it, "No way, Dad, I could never do such a terrible thing!"

Justin's dad looked him in the eye and said, "Son, one of the neighbors saw you go into the house the day it was flooded. Justin, I know it was you!" The boy began to sob. The jig was up. "Dad, I'm so sorry!! Ever since I flooded the house I've been dying inside!"

Well, Justin's father began to lay into his boy telling him that he was going to lose everything he loved for a while. Justin, broken by his shame, said, "Dad, I've been praying every night, asking Jesus to forgive me."

"What did you say?", dad asked.

Justin said it again, "Ever since I did that awful thing, I've been praying that Jesus would forgive me."

Dad responded, "Well, son, you didn't tell me that. I'm so glad to hear that. Now go out and play with your friends. I'll take care of this for you. I love you, son."

He fully absolved his son and sent him on his way. The father took full responsibility for the sin of his boy. Justin was free from blame and was treated as though he had never committed this awful act. Is this bad parenting? I don't know. What I am certain of is that Justin had been crushed under the weight of his guilt. He KNEW he had done a terrible thing. But dad set him free.

But wait. Shouldn't dad have given him some serious consequences? This was a spiteful and reckless thing Justin did. He needed to pay for his wrongs, don't you think? I don't know. Maybe. But his dad wanted to paint an important picture for his rebellious son.

This is a picture of what Jesus has done for you and me. We, who are guilty and deserve to pay, have been forgiven by our Father and declared NOT GUILTY.

It's not fair, is it? It sounds too good to be true! Well, friend, because the Gospel IS true, we live as dearly-loved children who have been set free from responsibility for the despicable things we've said, done and thought.

You might be like me. I have made a mess of things. I'm a drunk. I'm a fraud. I'm a hypocrite. I've ruined so many good things in my life. I'm a sin machine!! And Jesus knows all of it and more! Yet He loves me. Even when I do my best to cover up my wrongs, He loves me. When I take Him for granted, He loves me! He must be out of His mind...

Some people who read this chapter are concerned that grace that is taken too far will create lazy Christians who don't want to "grow in their faith" and serve the Lord. This is a common point of contention when talking about radical grace and its implications for broken sinners like you and me.

Tullian Tchividjian blows that argument up and I love it:

> *"A 'yes, grace...but' disposition is the kind of posture that keeps moralism swirling around in the church. Some of us think the only way to keep licentious people in line is by giving them the law.*

> *But the fact is, the only way licentious people start to obey is when they get a taste of God's radical acceptance of sinners. The more Jesus is held up as being sufficient for our justification and sanctification, the more we begin to die to ourselves and live to God. Those who end up obeying more are those who increasingly understand that their standing with God is not based on their obedience, but Christ's".* [1]

So because Jesus has taken full and final responsibility for your sin, go out and play with your friends! Live in the freedom that is now yours. Know that the grace of God covers everything you've ever done that you wish you could undo and so much more!

But don't forget to tell them what your Daddy did…

a prayer for today

Lord, may the reality of your one-way love for me rock my world today. I pray that the Gospel will so overwhelm me that I can't help but share it with those around me. This isn't my story anymore. It's the story of your work on the Cross for me. Make me glad, O God! May you fill my heart with your love today. And, Lord, may my life reflect the sweet good news that has saved me and changed me. Thanks, God, for loving me…

22
You Need More Than A Second Chance, You Know...

Years ago I was in a relationship with a girl named Joanie (not really her name). She was beautiful, smart, fun to be with and I thought she was the ONE! I was young, immature, cocky and self-absorbed. You can see we were good together, right!?

I was a youth pastor at the time and that season of my life was not an easy one. Things at the church were not going really well. I had a few parents who were gunning for me and I felt like I was constantly playing defense. I was still growing up and that didn't help. Joanie tried to be supportive and encouraging but she often bore the brunt of my job frustration. I was becoming a first-class jerk.

The rhythm of our relationship went like this: I'd go through a hard time. I'd project my frustration on to her. I'd apologize. She'd give me another chance to get it right. I'd promise to be a better boyfriend.

This continued for several months. As each month passed, Joanie got more and more discouraged. She wanted better. She deserved better! But she found herself in a no-win relationship with a boyfriend who didn't treat her very well. Joanie decided that she'd had enough.

She drove to my apartment one evening and told me that we were over. She was breaking up with me.

I begged her not to give up on me and to give me ONE MORE CHANCE. She said that there would be no more chances. She was done.

I spent most of my life believing that God was a God of second chances. Jesus died to give me another chance at life, or so I thought. I believed that the Gospel brought me a temporary reprieve and an opportunity to get it right. And because I kept getting it wrong, I'd run to the front of the church every time there was an altar call in hopes that God would give me one more chance to be faithful and committed enough to remain in His good graces. What a hopeless way to live!

Aaron Wilson sees it this way:

> *"Think of a kindergartner taking a calculus test. Because he's only 5, the little tyke bombs the test and receives an "F" atop his page. The teacher might show mercy, tear up his exam, and forgive his failure. But the lad will not rejoice when a fresh, identical test is placed in front of him for a second attempt. While some Mensa-in-waiting kindergartner might pass calculus, there's zero chance a fallen human can pass the test of God's law. As Scripture declares, 'None is righteous, no, not one' (Rom. 3:10). And since there's zero chance humans will obey God perfectly, why would Christians spread news of a God of second chances? Is it good news to get a second chance at the impossible?"* [1]

In Romans 6:9-11 we read, **"We know that Christ, being raised from the dead, will never die again; death no longer has dominion over him. For the death he died he died to sin, once for all, but the life he lives he lives to God. So you also must consider yourselves dead to sin and alive to God in Christ Jesus."**

Did you catch those three powerful words? ONCE FOR ALL. Those words were life-giving for me.

Jesus has made me alive, never to be dead in my sin ever again.

He has made me right with a holy God and there's nothing I can do to ever mess that up! He didn't die to buy me a temporary reprieve or a second chance at getting things right. He took my place. He took my sin and gave me the credit for His perfect performance.

God is not a God of second chances! He doesn't give us another chance to get it right or get it better. He gave us one chance and we blew it! Our sin rendered us helpless and hopeless. For you and me it was GAME OVER.

But because the Gospel is true, you and I who believe now live under a banner that says, "DONE!" We don't need another chance to get it right because Jesus got it right for us. And it drives me crazy when preachers fail to drive this home! I've heard so many "second chance" sermons that I want to scream. The Bible says that we needed more than a second chance. We needed rescue. And that's precisely what Jesus bought for us!

Deep down inside our hearts each one of us wants to hide the ugly, messy and broken parts of our lives. We fear rejection and condemnation from those around us. We want to be known, but what we really want is for the world to know a version of us that looks more 'together' than we really are. God knows us better than we know ourselves. He is well-acquainted with our mess and loves us nonetheless. He punished Jesus for our sin and counts us as fully righteous because of what took place at Calvary. Rest in that good news today, friend...

So today, know that you are not living your life having been given another chance to get things right so that you can stay in God's good graces. Jesus took care of that already. You've been made alive to God where you had once been dead in your sin. You're free now! So walk in that freedom, knowing that the pressure to perform is off. He loves you and you can't wreck that!

a prayer for today

I come to you with promises that I'll break, commitment that I won't follow through on, a dedication to get things right in my life and a passion that is prone to fade. You say, "Come to me empty-handed and trust that my finished work is enough. Leave your promises and commitments behind and receive from me. My grace and mercy come to you as a free gift with no strings attached."

Help me to believe this today, Lord...

23

You're More Desperate Than You Think...

As an alcoholic, I got to a place where I realized that my life had become unmanageable. I was completely out of control. I mean, I hadn't gotten any DUI's or anything, but I was absolutely powerless to stop drinking. That night when my wife found me drunk, I knew I needed help. I had to swallow my pride and find my way to a "meeting". I walked in the door of that place like a drowning man. I was desperate for help and I was ready to do anything to stop drinking. To me, this was a move of absolute desperation because I thought only people who were really messed up went to meetings like that. But I was desperate.

Desperate people do desperate things.

"And there was a woman who had had a discharge of blood for twelve years, and though she had spent all her living on physicians, she could not be healed by anyone. She came up behind him and touched the fringe of his garment, and immediately her discharge of blood ceased. And Jesus said, 'Who was it that touched me?' When all denied it, Peter said, 'Master, the crowds surround you and are pressing in on you!' But Jesus said, 'Someone touched me, for I perceive that power has gone out from me.' And when the woman saw that she was not hidden, she came trembling, and falling down before him declared in the presence of all the people why she had touched him, and how she had been immediately healed. And he said to her, 'Daughter, your faith has made you well; go in peace.'" Luke 8:43-48 ESV

This woman came to Jesus because she was desperate. She had no other hope. There were no more options for her. She was out of money and out of solutions. So, in her desperation, she went for it.

Desperate people do strange and sometimes unreasonable things. She certainly did. She pushed her way through the crowd as Jesus walked along a narrow dirt road, reached out and touched His shirt.

Like that would do anything, right! Her desperation made her look pretty pathetic.

But she found herself in an impossible situation and had to do SOMETHING.

The Bible says that you and I are in an impossible situation, too. We've been found guilty before God. We've broken His perfect Law and we've broken it BIG TIME! A holy God cannot accept even a hint of unrighteousness. Our sin makes Him sick! And the penalty for violating His Law: Death. We owe a debt that we can't even begin to pay back. For you and me, it's the worst news possible.

So there we sit in our own desperation, unable to maneuver our way out of the mess our sin has made. We deserve every ounce of condemnation that God promises to bring.

But Jesus paid the debt we owe. Someone had to pay, you know. God wasn't just going to give sinners a pass. Jesus took full and final responsibility for our sin. And when He rose from the dead, our debt slip was marked "PAID IN FULL". We would never again bear the burden of sin. We would never have to fear the condemnation of God. We are free and forgiven.

Like the woman in Scripture, we are faced with the reality of our sickness. And like her, we reach out in desperation hoping to find relief. By faith, she grabbed Jesus' shirt and the Bible says that she was made well. By faith we believe in a rescue plan that sounds too good to be true.

It's a plan authored by a Holy God who delights to show us mercy. The world thinks we are pathetic to believe in such a ridiculous plan. Karma sounds more equitable. Do good, get good. Do bad, get bad.

But grace is given to those who can acknowledge their desperation. For broken sinners like you and me, God went the whole way! He gave us His Son. It cost Him everything, yet it costs us nothing. It's true. Good news for desperate, broken people who believe in Him, trusting in His provision for us. We don't strike a deal with Him. No promises to do better or be better. All we bring to Him is our sin, because that's all we have. And He meets us with grace, mercy, love and acceptance FOREVER!

Brian Borgman talks about desperation as the great equalizer, even for pastors:

> "When we see ourselves as desperate sinners in need of the grace of Christ, it changes the way we look at others, what we expect of others, and what we want the church to be." [1]

I posted this on Facebook last year when the reality of who I was stared me in the face:

> "I have discovered again over the last week or so that I am more broken and messed up than I want to acknowledge to anyone. But God's grace fills my cup to overflow. He should be tired of me by now. He should have cast me aside for sure. But He remains faithful to me when I am faithless. He remains committed to me when my commitment wanes. He stubbornly refuses to stop loving me. What is he thinking!!!"

I wrote those words as a desperate man. They were hard to write but true for me. So today, remember your desperation. Remember the reality of what you deserve because of your sin. And then remember what He did to make you right with God. And thank Him for giving you the very faith to believe in Him.

See, I told you the news was good…for the desperate ones like you and me.

a prayer for today

God, please remind me that we come to you like drowning people, desperate for a rescue only you can provide. I cringe when I think about the judgment and condemnation I deserve.

But, Father, I rejoice in the Gospel today, which announces my total rescue because of Christ's work. Make me a grateful follower today, I pray. And thank you for the grace and mercy which will sustain me today...

24

Theology Of Glory Vs. Theology Of The Cross

I remember hearing a sermon years ago that troubled me. The pastor said, "Are you more like Jesus now than you were a year ago?" He then put a chart up on the screen that he urged the congregation to embrace. The chart was a type of measurement of spiritual growth. Lots of letters, numbers and lines. I left church that day shaking my head.

The problem with this chart was that it was supposed to measure my improvement and progress as a believer. It would paint a picture of how much my behavior had gotten better. It would also show me those areas that I had better address, and quick!

This is the theology of glory. It sees the cross as a necessary starting point for the believer but its significance is slowly downplayed in favor of a new symbol: A ladder. It's as though the cross was crucial to get me in the game but now I had better start climbing that ladder. And if I don't climb fast enough, I might be in trouble with God.

Tullian Tchividjian says it this way:

> *"The theology of glory is the natural default setting for human beings addicted to control and measurement. This perspective puts us squarely in the driver's seat, after all. In the church, one hallmark of a theology of glory is the unwillingness to acknowledge the reality of ongoing sin and lack of transformation in Christians. A sign that you are operating with a theology of glory is when your faith feels like a fight against these realities instead of a resource for accepting them."* [1]

I have discovered that, for me, my "progress" and "improvement" as a Christian has been pretty pitiful. Yes, the Holy Spirit is at work, reproducing the character of Christ in me. But that work is slow. You see, I am simultaneously SINNER and SAINT. And the tension that creates is real!

The Apostle Paul speaks for all of us when he writes:

"For I do not understand my own actions. For I do not do what I want, but I do the very thing I hate." Romans 7:15

People who embrace a theology of glory don't want to acknowledge this reality. Paul later admitted, "I am the worst of all sinners!" That doesn't sound like a guy who has improved a lot!!

A theology of the **cross** forces us to be honest about our sin, brokenness and need.

Martin Luther wrote, *"A Theologian of the Cross says what a thing is!"*

A theology of the cross defines the Christian life in terms of weakness rather than strength. And it's our weakness that drives us to the strong one – Jesus. He not only bore the weight of our sin, He remains strong when we fail and fall. And we do all the time…

Today, can I invite you to put the ladder away? In fact, don't just put it away, THROW it away! You don't need it anymore. It no longer symbolizes your life. Run to the cross where the rest of us weaklings are gathered. Join us! There's room for you.

Leave your improvement plan behind and rest in the unconditional love of your Savior. You can't mess this up! Your lack of progress will never cause Him to cast you aside. He will never stop pursuing you with His love.

Recently, I spoke with Dr. Steve Brown on our radio show. He said something profound that brought me great comfort and hope. He said, "The only people who ever 'get better' are the ones who know that if they don't, Jesus will still love and accept them."

This sweet news of the Gospel is not a call to be good or better. It announces that Jesus was good IN OUR PLACE! It doesn't come with a clause that requires something from us. It doesn't have fine print that binds you and me to a life of performance and growth. It comes to you and me with no strings attached. No conditions. Our standing with God is not dependent on our good life after receiving the Gospel. It is found within the Gospel itself.

Ray Ortlund describes the Gospel so powerfully:

> *"The gospel is not law, demanding that we pay our own way. The gospel is a welcome announcement, declaring that Jesus paid it all.*

It's like a long-awaited telephone call. When the phone finally rings, we grab the phone and eagerly take that call. This gospel is a message to be proclaimed and believed." [2]

Most evangelists hope to reach people outside the church. I want to be an evangelist for people INSIDE the church, who've missed the sweet good news of the Gospel. They see Jesus mostly as a coach rather than a Savior. They see him primarily as an example rather than a rescuer. They see their lives as an exercise in "do more, try harder"! They believe that it was Jesus' blood and sweat that got them God's acceptance but it's THEIR blood and sweat that keeps them in God's good graces. They hope that they can keep God from being mad at them by being good.

I want to reach the weary and the worn out with Good News of radical grace and mercy given by a God who loves broken and messed up people like me. Will you join me in spreading this GOOD NEWS?

a prayer for today

God, it's so easy to forget how much I really need you. Today I'll be tempted to think that I've grown out of my dependence on you for all things. Like a child needs his parents less and less as they grow up. Please don't let me believe that lie. "I need you. Every hour I need you. My one defense, my righteousness. Oh God, how I need you." And Lord, thank you for your promise to never grow tired of wanderers who gets it so wrong, so often. I need you today...

25
I'm Not Sure I'd Pass That Test...

April 20, 1999 is a day many Americans won't forget. In Littleton, Colorado, two students brought weapons to their high school and went on a rampage killing 15, and injuring 24. Eric Harris and Dylan Klebold wanted their attack to rival the Oklahoma City bombing. As a nation we mourned in disbelief...

Shortly after the attack, we heard a story about a student named Cassie Bernall, who was killed while hiding in the library with other students. The story was told that Klebold entered the library, approached Cassie and asked, "Do you believe in God?" She said, "Yes" and was immediately shot to death. The implication was that if she had denied faith in God she would have been spared. Cassie Bernall was championed as a Christian martyr who was gunned down for her faith. She was given a test and she passed it.

It was determined later that this account was inaccurate. Cassie was, in fact, not given the chance to save herself by denying God. She was never asked about her belief in God at all. The shooter looked under a table where she was hiding with another girl and said, "Peekaboo" before shooting her. I don't write this to dishonor her memory. Her death was tragic and heartbreaking for many.

In the wake of the tragedy and Cassie's "story", many asked the question, "What would you do if you were given the 'test' that Cassie Bernall was given? Would you affirm your faith in Christ or would you deny knowing him, if it meant saving your life?"

So to be fair, the test was not actually given to Cassie, but what if it was? What if you and I were pressured at gunpoint to deny Him? How would you respond? Would you take the bullet?

I'm pretty sure that there are a lot of youth pastors who will tell their kids that this kind of bravery truly defines the Christian. To be a coward in a situation like this is to deny your Savior. "Real sold-out Christ followers would take that bullet in the name of Jesus!", they'd say.

On the night that Jesus was betrayed, we read:

And when they had sung a hymn, they went out to the Mount of Olives. Then Jesus said to them, "You will all fall away because of me this night. For it is written, 'I will strike the shepherd, and the sheep of the flock will be scattered.' But after I am raised up, I will go before you to Galilee." Peter answered him, "Though they all fall away because of you, I will never fall away." Jesus said to him, "Truly, I tell you, this very night, before the rooster crows, you will deny me three times." Peter said to him, "Even if I must die with you, I will not deny you!" And all the disciples said the same. Matthew 26-33-35 ESV

During the next several hours, Peter did just as Jesus said, despite his statement of commitment and dedication to His lord. He walked with Jesus during the years of His ministry, saw Him perform miracles, experienced His power, hung out with Him as a friend/confidant and STILL denied Him three times! Come on, Peter!! Jesus should have slayed and fileted you! What a horrible Christ-follower…He failed the test miserably.

I can only imagine the shame and regret that Peter felt, knowing that He had let down His friend. It wouldn't surprise me if Peter contemplated suicide after that ridiculous failure. He didn't just deny knowing one of his friends or neighbors, He denied knowing JESUS! Talk about a moral failure! He was given the test and, as Jesus foretold, He failed it epically.

Yet, we read about Jesus and Peter having breakfast together days later. Instead of letting him have it, Jesus reinstated Peter, showing great mercy to the denier. He invited the failed disciple to be part of a world-changing mission. What was He thinking?? Shouldn't Jesus have sent Peter away in exile for a while before welcoming him back to the fold? He needed to pay for his failure, don't you think? Well, shortly after his fall, Peter would preach the Gospel and thousands came to faith!

If confronted by a gunman who asked me, "Do you believe in God?" I hope I would take the right stand. But the reality is this: I love my life, my wife, my family and I know that if faced with death, in my weakness, I might choose them. That sounds very un-Christian, I know. But I'm a weakling. I need a Savior and He lived, died and rose again for weaklings like me.

Because the Gospel is true, I live knowing that it's His refusal to deny ME that secures my standing with God - forever! He passed the test and I get the credit for it! So do you, if you are trusting in Jesus' finished work on your behalf. This is good news that I pray brings relief to you. The Gospel isn't simply the beginning of a lifelong test that we either pass or fail. It is the good news that Jesus got an A and credits it to us! In fact in Christianity, we get the A before we do a single thing!

Today, you will be given the opportunity to identify with Christ. I hope and pray that you will. But, if in weakness you don't, know that His love will not fail to cover you. His grace and mercy are yours! His love for you cannot be disobeyed away! And that may be reason enough to say to the world, "I AM HIS, AND HE IS MINE!"

a prayer for today

I am becoming even more aware of my brokenness. The reality of my messy heart is sobering. At times I wanted to hide in shame. But Jesus, you bore my sin and shame, taking full and final responsibility for all of it. You died to address the ugly reality of my brokenness. And all that you did for me, you did gladly! So now when I look deep into my messy heart, I see the Cross. You love me THAT MUCH! The Gospel is such good news...

26

Stop Trying To Have A Relationship With God!

OK, so before you push back against the title of this chapter, give it a read and try to see where I'm coming from…

A few years ago I talked with a friend whose daughter had just gotten back from church camp. I asked how it was for her and she responded, "My daughter went to camp and began a relationship with God!"

It's a phrase that I hear a lot: A relationship with God. I've used it a ton in my own life and ministry. It sounds really good. A relationship with the Creator of the Universe – wow! So many pastors, Sunday school teachers, bible study leaders and speakers describe Christianity in relational terms. And it makes sense. We are relational people.

But as I grow in my understanding of the Scriptures, I am getting increasingly uncomfortable with this language.

What do we know about relationships? They take a lot of work! And if we don't nurture them and invest in them, we'll lose them.

I can't even begin to count the number of relationships I've lost over the years because I didn't do the work necessary to maintain them.

There really is no such thing as a one-way relationship. It must be about the mutual meeting of needs.

In our pre-marital counseling, my wife Larisa and I were challenged to never quit investing in each other. That meant carving out time to be together. It meant committing to make sure that nothing else took priority over our marriage relationship. And this was good advice that has kept us growing together for more than 20 years.

But what would happen to us if I stopped working at being a good husband? What if I stopped making time for her? What if I allowed others in my life to become more important than her? Do you think Larisa would stay with me if I were repeatedly unfaithful to her? If I became a husband who never talked with her or listened to her, do you think she'd stay with me?

No, I think she'd give up on our relationship at some point. I wouldn't blame her.

When we reduce God to someone we simply "relate to", we make a big mistake. The Gospel is not the good news that we can know and hang out with God if we want to. It's the proclamation to broken sinners that Jesus did for us what we couldn't do for ourselves! The Gospel announces that we who can't possibly be faithful enough to gain God's acceptance have been declared forgiven and fully accepted by God, once and for all.

When we try to make the wonder of Christianity something we can understand – like being in a relationship, we get ourselves into trouble. Because if we think that our standing with God is based on how much we're doing to maintain a good relationship with Him, we will find ourselves back on the treadmill of performance, hoping that we're investing enough of ourselves in the "relationship" In fact nowhere in the Bible do we see our salvation described in relational terms. Relationships are about two people with mutual commitment to one another, meeting one another's needs. The success of a relationship is rooted in doing enough, loving enough, caring enough, and being faithful enough. I'm not capable of this and neither are you. That's why there had to a cross!

Professor John Suk sees it this way, and I agree:

> *"Rather than saying, 'I have a personal relationship with Jesus,' why don't we say instead, 'I have faith in Jesus,' or 'I believe in Jesus.' Where the language of personal relationship has a very questionable pedigree, amidst a therapeutic culture, to cut God down to a manageable size, the language of faith is deeply rooted in Scripture."* [1]

NOW, because we who are broken are, by faith, trusting in Christ's finished work on our behalf, we are free to relate with Him. We are free to love Him and walk with Him – in messy and imperfect ways.

And His love for us is in no way based on our commitment to that relationship. If you are in Christ there is no need for you to question your standing with God because of things you've done or not done.

Today, you will be tempted to think that God is mad at you because of the ways you've failed Him. And make no mistake – you will absolutely fail Him. But His commitment to you is not a response to your commitment to Him. If you are in Christ, you can breathe. It's HIS faithfulness that makes your relationship with Him secure. It's His job to sustain you in the faith. His grace is given to you so that you will never have to bear the burden of performance ever again.

a prayer for today

Thank you Jesus for becoming one of us - and not just for a "visit" from Heaven. You came on a mission: You lived the life that I couldn't. You died the death that I deserved. You took my sin upon yourself and gave to me YOUR PERFECT RECORD of righteousness. I want to know you. I want to walk with you. I want to have a "relationship" with you. Remind me of your never-ending love and grace, oh Lord. I forget so easily. Remind me again that I'm yours and that there is really nothing I can do to wreck that!

27
Jim Carrey Gets It!

At the 2016 Golden Globes, actor and comedian Jim Carrey stepped forward to present the award for Best Musical or Comedy. It was his first public appearance since the death of his girlfriend.

"Thank you, I am two-time Golden Globe winner, Jim Carrey!"

"You know, when I go to sleep at night, I'm not just a guy going to sleep. I'm two-time Golden Globe winner Jim Carrey going to get some well-needed shut-eye".

The audience laughed loudly.

"When I dream I don't just dream any old dream. I dream about being three-time Golden Globe actor Jim Carrey. Because then I would be enough! It would finally be true, and I could stop this terrible search, for what I know ultimately won't fulfill me."

Jim Carrey had achieved almost everything that he had ever desired. He had tens of millions in the bank. He had a long string of box office hits. In so many ways, he had reached the pinnacle of success. And yet, he acknowledged before his Hollywood peers and the watching world that all of it left him feeling unfulfilled. He described a search for something that was missing.

On our show, we talk a lot about our "If Only's". If only I had a husband who was the spiritual leader that my pastor is.

If only we could live in that development across town that my wealthier friends live in. If only my kids would be like "so and so's kids", I could feel like a good mom. If only we could travel the world like my sister and her husband do? If only...

The Apostle Paul wrote these words:

"For the Kingdom of God is not a matter of eating and drinking, but of righteousness and peace and joy in the Holy Spirit." Romans 14:17 ESV

For those of us who are trusting in Christ, our fulfillment is found in something outside of ourselves. Having it all and being it all will only leave us unsatisfied. But the gifts that God gives us in Jesus are the very things that make us whole.

I have tried to find fulfillment in so many of the wrong things. I thought that if I were successful professionally I would be fulfilled. I believed that if I found the right person to spend my life with I would feel better about myself. I lived my life for many years thinking that if I were a good Christian, God would love me a little bit more and bless me just a little bit more. Surely, that would leave me feeling fulfilled.

I think Jim Carrey is right. We are all on a journey hoping to find that one thing that will leave us feeling satisfied. And that journey can leave us feeling weary and worn out. Then we get discouraged and then we begin to doubt everything. That weariness has led more than a few celebrities committing suicide.

There are many things that we look to for satisfaction that are less than Jesus. We hope that by succeeding in our careers we will be fulfilled. It is our hope that we can raise a family with no dark secrets and kids that turn out well, because certainly THAT will satisfy us. We put our hope in our ability to get our lives together. And what we discover is this: Only Jesus can really satisfy your soul.

The Gospel announces that Jesus has done everything that needs to be done to secure our hope.

We don't need to search the world over to find true satisfaction and fulfillment. His finished work has purchased for us the unconditional approval of Almighty God. In Christ, we are given everything that we will ever need! This is why the Gospel is called the GOOD NEWS! We don't need to go searching for that next trophy to make us feel like we've found that place of true satisfaction. God says to you and me that everything that isn't Him will leave us wanting.

The Bible has something to say about satisfaction, and it's born out of our gratitude for Him and His work in us:

As the deer longs for streams of water, so I long for you, O God. I thirst for God, the living God. When can I go and stand before him? Psalm 42:1-2

JD Greear surmises that many of us are looking for significance in the busyness of our lives:

"Jesus shatters the myth that busyness equals faithfulness; he confronts all of our fears that lead to our busyness, then he points us to a better way forward—resting in him. We sit at the feet of Jesus, find our sufficiency in him, and only then fill our schedules with whatever he tells us." [1]

So today, when you find yourself looking for that thing that will leave you feeling satisfied and fulfilled, preach the Gospel to yourself and be reminded of His love for you. It's a love that saves, transforms and secures our standing with Him!

Your search can truly be over, friend…

a prayer for today

God, please help me to trust you today. It's so easy to think that I know best, but we both know that's messed up. Your promises are true, but sometimes I struggle to believe that they're true for ME. I don't understand why you stay faithful to me when I am so unfaithful to you. Thank you for the forgiveness of my sin and the righteousness that I'm given in Christ. May that reality blow my mind a bit when I doubt you. Thanks for loving this flaky follower…

28

Reputations

They say that your reputation is what other people think and say about you. It's based on your history – the things you've said, done and left undone. Some reputations are earned over many years. Still others are earned after limited time spent with you. A reputation is not something that you can give yourself, no matter how hard you try. It's all about others and the impression you've left on them.

In some circles I have a very good reputation. I talk to 400,000 people on the radio in Dallas-Ft. Worth each morning and based on our success as a show, I'd say that my reputation seems to be pretty solid. In order to do what I do, you have to get people to like you. They have lots of options on the dial and if they don't like you they can easily find another morning show. I'm told that I have a reputation for talking about grace. I'm told that I have a reputation for sometimes being the "brat" on our show. I'm good with that.

All that said, I can tell you that there are lots and lots of people who would say that I have a really bad reputation. They'll tell you that I often speak without thinking. They will probably list some of my less-than-desirable qualities and how those qualities have gotten me in trouble. They'll certainly tell you about the wreckage I've left behind because I'm a broken mess of a guy. I've burned a lot of bridges in my life and I'm not proud that my reputation has suffered greatly because of things I've said and done that have hurt others.

And come on – I'm an alcoholic. That fact has affected my reputation in profound ways.

I'm known by some as the guy with no self-control whatsoever. Others see me as the selfish guy who chose whiskey, rum and vodka over his family. And yes, there are people who have said, "I knew something like this would happen to him!"

My reputation has cost me jobs I was trying to get. There were women I wanted to date that wouldn't let me near them because of my reputation. I've walked in on conversations that people were having about what a jerk I was. Writing all this makes me cringe a little, if I'm being honest. Looking back, I deserved all of it.

It got so bad for me that I used to have a post-it note stuck to my computer monitor at work with a current list of "People Who Are Ticked Off At Jeff". That list needed updating far too often.

Listen to what some interesting people say about reputations:

> "It takes 20 years to build a reputation and five minutes to ruin it. If you think about that, you'll do things differently."
>
> *-Warren Buffett*

"Me, I'd prefer to have a good reputation rather than getting press for being scandalous, getting drunk in public, staying out late and so on."

-Actress Sophia Bush

"Partly, I like a bad reputation. But I also want a reputation of being a good person."

-Singer Joan Jett

"Be more concerned with your character than your reputation."

-Coach John Wooden [1]

The Bible says that because of our sin each of us has a "bad reputation" spiritually-speaking. Our inability to meet God's holy demands has rendered us helpless and hopeless. God looks at our sin and it literally makes Him sick! We are so sin-soaked that His Word tells us that there is nothing good in us.

But maybe you're thinking that you're a pretty good person who works hard, helps others, gives to worthy causes, doesn't use bad language and maybe even attends church regularly. Surely you don't deserve to be described in the terms I just cited.

The Bible describes us in terms that are hard to hear. They diagnose a condition that plagues every human being who has ever lived – except one. In God's economy, our reputations are so not good. The Apostle Paul writes this indictment of mankind.

"As the Scriptures say, 'No one is righteous—not even one. No one is truly wise; no one is seeking God. All have turned

away; All have become useless. No one does good, not a single one.'" Romans 3:10-12 NLT

This is who we are. And it gets even worse. Our "reputation" before God earns us one big fat ugly thing: CONDEMNATION. Like I've said several times in this little book, for you and me who are sin-sick it's GAME OVER.

But this is precisely why Jesus came. It took someone with a perfect reputation to stand in our place. Jesus lived the righteous life that God demanded of us. Not only did He die to take full and final responsibility for our sin, He gives us His righteousness. His reputation is now ours. And our sin-soaked reputations are taken from us, never to be held over our heads ever again.

If I could go back and undo some of the damage I have done that has resulted in a less-than-stellar reputation, I would. Do I have regrets and will I live with them until I die? Yes. Will your failures be held against you by others – possibly for a very long time? Probably. But God will never again speak of your wrongs if you are trusting in Jesus. He will look at you and only see the perfect reputation of His righteous Son, who took your place once and for all.

His grace really is enough to cover even the worst reputations. That's good news for guys like me...

a prayer for today

God, I have hurt others and I wish I could undo all of it. I have said and done things that I regret and my heart hurts when I think about the wreckage I have left behind. Forgive me, please, for a reputation that isn't as good as I'd like it to be. Because of the Cross, you have traded places with me and that brings comfort and relief to me today. I pray, Lord, that your Holy Spirit would do a work in me, reproducing the character of Christ in me. Bless me today, God…

29
But Why Did He Have To DIE?

In the early 1980's I was a staff member with Young Life in Southwest Florida. These were formative years and helped lay the groundwork for many subsequent years spent in youth ministry. In addition to two different weekly gatherings with kids, I spent my time in relational-incarnational ministry to teenagers. I lived my life among the ones I wanted to reach with the Gospel.

Each summer, we took twenty-five kids to Young Life camp in North Carolina. Windy Gap was a fantastic camp that sat surrounded by the Blue Ridge Mountains. Many of our YL kids came to know Jesus at camp.

In 1984, we took a group of kids to Windy Gap that included a boy named David. I didn't know him well when we left for camp, but soon David and I struck up a friendship. He came from a broken home and was very resistant to anything having to do with religion. He said to me, "It all seems so pointless."

On the fifth night of camp, the speaker shared the message of the Cross. It was a clear, relatable and powerful talk. The reality of our sin and the subsequent necessity of the Cross really hit home for many of our kids that night. It hit home for me, too.

Immediately following that message, the students were told that camp was going to shutdown for 20 minutes. No activities, no snack shop, no nothing.

The speaker asked the kids to observe 20 minutes of silence. They were instructed to go and find a place on the grounds to be alone – to think about the talk they had just heard. Those 20 minutes were powerful.

I was walking around the camp grounds as kids sat alone contemplating the cross and as I did, I saw David. He was sitting under a tree sobbing. It was as though tears were literally flying out of his face. I walked over to him to see if he was ok. Through the tears he cried out to me, "WHY DID HE HAVE TO DIE??!!!" The dark reality of the slain Son of God rocked David's world and broke His heart. I started to cry, too.

I looked at him and said, "David, it was because of you…and me. Your sin and my sin put Him on that cross." We talked about our sin that forced Jesus to loving action on our behalf. David cried and cried as the sweet reality of the Cross washed over him. That night I led David to the Lord, but I prefer to look at it this way: I witnessed his conversion. Yes, I saw the power of the Gospel cut to the heart of a boy who had, for the first time, come face-to-face with his sin. The love of God became real to an 11th grade boy that night.

For you and me, it matters so much that we come to the same realization that it was our sin and rebellion that nailed Him to that Cross. The bible says that you and I are enemies of God. Our sin and brokenness separate us from Him. There is no hope for us because our sin problem is that bad. Peace between us and God is impossible without first addressing our wretchedness.

But in Colossians we read:

"For in Him all the fullness of God was pleased to dwell, and through Him to reconcile to himself all things, whether on earth or in heaven, making peace by the blood of His cross." Colossians 1:19-20 ESV

That night, as David sat under that tree, he was brought to a place to which we all must go.

He realized for the first time that HE was responsible for Christ's death. It was our sin that put Him up on that awful cross. And yet, He went there gladly. And if you were the only sinner that needed saving, He'd have died for you.

Bryan Chapell tells this story and what a picture it paints:

> *"On August 16, 1987, Northwest Airlines flight 225 crashed just after taking off from Detroit, killing 155 people. One survived: a four-year-old from Arizona named Cecelia.*
>
> *News accounts say when rescuers found Cecelia they did not believe she had been on the plane. Investigators first assumed Cecelia had been a passenger in one of the cars on the highway onto which the airliner crashed.*
>
> *But when the passenger register for the flight was checked, there was Cecelia's name. Cecelia survived because, even as the plane was falling, Cecelia's mother, Paula Chican, unbuckled her own seat belt, got down in front of her, wrapped her arms and body around Cecelia, and then would not let her go.*

Nothing could separate that child from her parent's love—neither tragedy nor disaster, neither the fall nor the flames that followed, neither height nor depth, neither life nor death. Such is the love of our Savior for us. He left heaven, lowered himself to us, and covered us with the sacrifice of his own body to save us." [1]

Today, you will be tempted to believe that you aren't really that bad. It's a lie. You are way worse than you think. But you are more deeply-loved by God than you could ever dare hope. It was for you that He sacrificed His Son. Rest in that and allow that sweet news to change your heart.

a prayer for today

Lord, it's so easy to get caught in the trap of comparison. I pray that you'll help me to not compare myself to those around me. Keep me from feeling "less than" when I see how put together others seem to be. But, Lord, keep me from feeling better about myself when I see the struggles that others face. Remind me today that my identity is anchored in who YOU say that I am. And may that be enough...

30

What Are You Trying To Accomplish?

I was thinking about my upcoming funeral the other day! Really, I was. I'm not sure when it will occur, but one day, I will die. Shortly afterward, my friends and family will gather to mourn together. I will be there in body, but not in Spirit.

At most of the funerals that I have attended, they pass out a program that includes the order of the service and a eulogy. It's the eulogy that has me thinking. The eulogy is a condensed story of a person's life. It highlights the major events and accomplishments of the deceased.

My eulogy, I imagine, will be a white-washed version of my story. It won't be laced with lists of my accomplishments because I haven't had all that many. Don't get me wrong, I have had a few victories in my life. But my "trophy case" is pretty bare. My list of failures is much longer. I suspect, though, that no one will care to mention any of them at my funeral.

One day, I will stand before God and be judged by Him. You will, too. I know a lot of people who fear that day. They hope that by the time they get there, they will have done enough to be approved by God. Even now, they live afraid of what that final verdict will be.

When they imagine Judgment Day, they tremble as they contemplate questions like these:

1. *Was I faithful enough?*

2. *Was I committed enough?*

3. *Did I walk closely enough with God?*

4. *Did I spend enough time in church?*

5. *Did my good works outweigh my bad decisions?*

6. *Did I accomplish enough with the life I was given?*

I have written this book especially for people who ask these questions. I mean, we all ask these questions because we really and truly hope that we have accomplished enough in this life.

Thankfully, for those of us who are in Christ, our Judgment Day has already taken place! Jesus was judged for your sin and mine, and, as I have said many times in this book, He took full and final responsibility for our sin! Double Jeopardy applies here, you know. God will not judge you for the sin in your life when He has already convicted His Son for it.

God's Law demands that each of us be judged by the accomplishments we have achieved. The Gospel announces that you and I are now judged on the sum of Christ's accomplishments. Our sin was given to Him and His perfect record has been applied to our account, ONCE AND FOR ALL!! We are the righteousness of God!

Hear what Robert Kolb has to say about what righteousness means for us now:

> *"Sanctification is not a process whereby we move from 57 percent holy to 58 percent holy. The Christian is 100 percent holy and now tries to manifest that righteousness, to make it known in daily life, in spite of the resistance of sin. Faith grows as it breaks free from its bonds of encumbering sin."* [1]

Today you will be given the chance to accomplish. I hope you accomplish a lot! But please remember that your standing with God is secure because of Christ's accomplishments and not yours.

Your "trophy case" might be a bit bare, but Jesus has the most well-stocked collection of accomplishments ever, and your name is on every trophy and award. How does THAT sound?

Live this day with freedom and confidence knowing that your Savior loves you and has provided for you. The burden of sin has been lifted and you can walk easier without the weight of that ugliness slowing you down.

It's been said that an unbelieving world wants to see that we Christians are "the real deal". Well, I don't know about you but I am absolutely NOT the real deal. I'm a flaky follower who struggles with brokenness. I'm prone to wander - to leave the God I love. If the world wants to see that I'm the real deal in order to believe, no one will ever come to faith. Thankfully, Jesus

IS the real deal. His grace and mercy for sinners like you and me - WOW! Don't look at me...look at Him!

Nothing has motivated me more to serve the Lord with my life than the reality of the Gospel! I soak in the good news of radical grace each day and it both comforts me AND transforms me. Rules and finger-waving messages didn't move me. But the reminder of His great unconditional love and acceptance DO move me! The Gospel is so good...

Go in peace, my friend...

a prayer for today

God, I need you. I don't want to deal with the stuff of this day by myself. Thanks, Lord, because you have promised to walk beside me. But I need you to LEAD me today. I want to walk in step with you. But I know myself and I am prone go my own way. Please keep me from wandering too far from you. Thanks in advance for the grace I'll need today.

31

The Perfect Church

Lisa is a friend of mine who grew up in church. Hers was a small church and Lisa liked it that way. She knew everyone there and they knew her. In her mind, she belonged to the perfect church. But as Lisa grew into adulthood, she began to see past the masks that everyone wore. She began to see the hypocrisy and that left her feeling quite disillusioned. Slowly, she drifted away and never came back.

You probably know someone like Lisa. Maybe you ARE someone like Lisa. Many people have become disillusioned by what they have seen and experienced in church. They rail against the Pharisaical attitudes, the judgmental spirit, and the hypocrisy.

If I could sit down with Lisa and share my heart with her, I'd want her to know that I get it. I've seen all the yuckiness in church, too, and it makes me sad. I'd tell her that all the un-Christian stuff she's seen in her church can be found in EVERY church. Jesus encountered all kinds of hypocrisy...

"Early in the morning he came again to the temple. All the people came to him, and he sat down and taught them. The scribes and the Pharisees brought a woman who had been caught in adultery, and placing her in the midst they said to him, 'Teacher, this woman has been caught in the act of adultery. Now in the Law Moses commanded us to stone such women. So what do you say?'

This they said to test him, that they might have some charge to bring against him. Jesus bent down and wrote with his finger on the ground. And as they continued to ask him, he stood up and said to them, 'Let him who is without sin among you be the first to throw a stone at her.' And once more he bent down and wrote on the ground. But when they heard it, they went away one by one, beginning with the older ones, and Jesus was left alone with the woman standing before him. Jesus stood up and said to her, 'Woman, where are they? Has no one condemned you?' She said, 'No one, Lord.' And Jesus said, 'Neither do I condemn you; go, and from now on sin no more." John 8:2-11 ESV

When confronted by the hypocritical church folks of His day, Jesus showed grace and mercy. And not just to the woman who had been caught in adultery, but to the hypocrites themselves. Seriously, He could have heaved stones at all of them because of their unrighteousness! Yes, He confronted them – but I think He did it by holding a mirror up for them to see themselves for who they were. I mean, He went to the cross for them, too.

I am broken. I am a fraud. I am a hypocrite. So are you.

But what kind of hypocrite will you be? Will you allow the truth of your hypocrisy to drive you to the Savior who freely gives us grace, mercy and forgiveness? Or will you become self-righteous, believing that you aren't really that bad – that somehow because you're a Christian you are a little bit better than everyone else.

Your church is filled with frauds, scoundrels, cheaters and misfits. Mine is, too. There is no perfect church! And as someone once said, "If you find the perfect church, don't go there, because you'll mess it up!"

Churches are filled with broken and messed up people. That's ALL of us! What if church looked more like a recovery meeting of strugglers and less like a rock concert?

What if we could be honest about our failures and doubts, knowing that we were in good company as we seek to know the truth of His love? How might we love each other more richly if we knew how sick each of us is?

Sadly, I have attended some of the largest and best-known churches in America and while they bring tremendous creativity, passion, and innovation to the worship experience, something is often missing: The Gospel. In some churches the Gospel gets a nod once in a while but the desire to make the Bible relevant has resulted in the abandonment of the simple good news of Christ's substitutionary atonement. Maybe they think people are coming to learn how to have a better and more fulfilling life. Sadly, worshippers get lists, plans and advice about life from the Bible, but no Gospel.

If the church has left you feeling discouraged and disillusioned, take heart. The church is not a museum for the saints. It's a hospital for the broken, weary and wounded. And hopefully, it's a place where your hypocrisy will be met with God's radical grace. You're not alone, you know.

Jared Wilson says this:

> *"If the Gospel is being regularly preached in your church, you will eventually become a magnet for the messiest kind of sinners."* [1]

I want to be part of THAT kind of church…

a prayer for today

Lord, may the Gospel captivate me in a fresh new way today. May your love and grace for broken people like me WOW me. You pursue me with your love and for that I'm so grateful. Help me to not wander as I navigate this day. Keep my eyes on you and help me to reflect your love to others who are as in need of your love as I am. And when things get stressful and tense, remind me that you are with me in everything, Lord. Thanks for your provision and your presence.

32

My Story

Hi, I'm Jeff and I'm an alcoholic.

During a very difficult time in my life back in 2004, I began to abuse alcohol. I believed that self-medicating would help ease the pain from a heart that was broken. I won't get into all the things that were happening in my life at that time, but booze became my dear friend.

I think I believed that God had gotten it wrong and allowed me to end up on the short end of life. Surely He had forgotten me. You see, the circumstances of that time were more than I could bear alone. So I drank. Oh yes, I drank.

Over the next six years, I grew more and more dependent on alcohol and became a really heavy drinker. I literally drank myself to sleep every night for more than half a decade. When my wife confronted me about it, I lied. I hid my bottles of whisky, rum, vodka and wine and did my drinking in secret. I mean, after all, that's what drunks do.

Between 2004 and 2010, I quit drinking hundreds of times, only to rationalize a few more drinks the next day, promising myself that I would quit tomorrow. I had become an alcoholic and my life was spinning out of control.

On July 4th, 2010, I sat alone in church while my family was away on a trip. In that seat in the third row, I quietly cried out to God asking Him to rescue me. I needed Him to be real for me. He delivered. As I sat there crying out to Him, "I was overcome by these words that I believe God spoke to my heart: I'VE GOT THIS.

That day, my abuse of alcohol stopped. Not because I decided it was time, but because God was giving me what I needed to live differently. My sobriety has not been without hiccups and I know first-hand what relapse is about, but God is daily giving me the strength to trust Him as I navigate the world without getting drunk each day.

But here's the thing, friend. I am so perfectly loved by God that even if I fall completely off the wagon and become a raging drunk once again, God will not withhold His love from me. He won't say, "Jeff, you stupid, ungrateful fool! Don't you know that I died for you and gave you the power to live without alcohol? You know better and you still choose to be a drunk! Well, mister, that's it! I'm done with you!! Come see me when you're really ready to get it together. Until then, I am out of here!"

No. God has promised me that He will never leave me nor forsake me! I am secure in His love and acceptance that Jesus won for me on the Cross. And knowing that makes me grateful. So grateful, that I want to live for Him! So grateful that I want to know Him, love Him and serve Him. But I so quickly default to rule-keeping if I'm not focused on the Gospel.

Gavin Ortlund, has this to say about our new lives as believers:

> "However much we may laud grace with our lips, our hearts are so thoroughly law-marinated that the Christian life must be, at core, one of continually bathing our hearts and minds in gospel grace. We are addicted to law. Conforming our lives to a moral framework, playing by the rules, meeting a minimum standard—this feels normal.
>
> And it is how we naturally medicate that deep sense of inadequacy within. The real question is not how to avoid becoming a Pharisee; the question is how to recover from being the Pharisee we already, from the womb, are." [1]

I'm not sure what demons you have. I don't know what your struggle looks like. But I do know that what Jesus did on the cross He did for you. He died to make things right between you and God. Your ability to hold it together no longer has any bearing on your good standing with Him. That's good news, right?

Bask in His love today. Let His power give you strength to live in a new way. Allow His love to overwhelm you so that your natural response would be to love Him right back! It's His grace that sustains us and motivates us.

Jerry Bridges wrote:

> "Only when we're thoroughly convinced that the Christian life is entirely of grace are we able to serve God out of a grateful and loving heart" [2]

While in the throws of my battle with alcohol, I was a drunk, a liar and a fraud. I asked my wife why she didn't leave me or kick me out until I got my life under control. She said it never entered her mind. You see, when you've been captivated by God's grace, it's so much easier to be gracious to the broken people in our lives. Even when we broken people drive ourselves into the ditch, God promises to never leave us and to be gracious to us.

When you fail and fall, He won't cut ties with you. He won't give up on you. Nothing can disqualify you from being His dearly-loved child. God will never abandon you out of frustration. He will never regret choosing to love and save you. His pursuit of you will continue even when you take His love for granted. Let that change your heart today, friend.

Things that don't make me a Christian

1. Putting Jesus #1 in my life

2. Committing to serve Him all the days of my life

3. Giving myself completely to Him

4. Promising to make Him Lord of my life

I am a Christian because of His finished work on the Cross. My standing with Him has everything to do with His commitment to sinners and His radical grace given to broken and messed up people like me. We are the receivers!

33
It's The Bomb-Diggity!

My wife's sister and her family live in Minot, ND. They purchased a home that was built in 1964 and it has a very unique feature: a bomb shelter. It has 12" concrete walls and ceilings and it was put in during the height of the Cold War. You see, Minot has a nuclear missile base close by and I guess that makes this area a bit of a hot spot in terms of potential attack. The more I think about it, a bomb shelter seems like a decent idea.

Now, I know that some may think that people who build shelters are paranoid. I'm not so sure. The idea of having a safe place to go in the event of a crisis sounds like a pretty good thing to me.

When I think about my life, I sometimes get a sense of anxiety. You see, I am a very great sinner and like the Apostle Paul, everything I want to do, I don't do. And everything I don't want to do, I do. The Bible has very serious words for people like you and me who are sin-soaked: Judgment, condemnation, death, eternal separation, and Hell.

I might look good and spiritual on the outside but in my heart, I am a wretched man.

When you look in the spiritual mirror of God's Word and you see who you really are, it can leave you feeling hopeless – wanting to hide from the world. The reality of our sin-sick selves can make us want to retreat to a place of acceptance and refuge, but there is no such place. There is nowhere to hide.

But Jesus came to do for us what we couldn't do for ourselves. He came to redeem broken sinners who have no place of refuge. He came to forgive and to heal broken lives. He came to give wretched people like you and me a place to rest, knowing that it was God himself who did all the redemption work.

In the book of Nahum we read:

"The Lord is good, a stronghold in the day of trouble; he knows those who take refuge in Him." Nahum 1:7

Because of Christ's finished work, we now are free to take refuge in God's love knowing that there is nothing we can do to mess it up. We can't out sin the coverage of His cross. We no longer have to live in fear when we see ourselves in the spiritual mirror of God's Word. Jesus says to you and me, "I know you better than you know yourself. I see the sin and the brokenness that once defined you. But take heart, I took responsibility for all of it!"

Jesus has provided for you and me a "spiritual bomb shelter" where we can take refuge from God's judgment and condemnation, because in Christ, we will never face them EVER! He's not saving a little for us just in case we get out of line and wander into the weeds.

I pray today that you will look at yourself in the mirror of God's Word and feel the weight of your sin problem. I hope that you will be rocked by the reality of God's condemnation of sinners like you and me. But most importantly, I pray that you will receive God's forgiveness, won for you by Jesus himself. In Christ, you have a new identity. No longer does your sin define you. Your identity is now anchored in who HE says you are. And He calls you His dearly-loved child.

Life can and will make for troubling seasons. Maybe you're in one right now. You desperately want to hide in a bunker until the battle is over. Well, because the Gospel is true, you and I can hide ourselves in Him.

"Keep me as the apple of your eye; hide me in the shadow of your wings." Psalm 17:8 NLT

Though the arrows fly, we can rest in His love and provision. He is there with us, even though we feel like we're the only ones who struggle in the way we do. And He is actively working for our best and for His glory.

But Paul Tripp says we have to be careful that we don't just seek any old refuge:

> *"Running and hiding doesn't get us into trouble; running to the wrong refuge and hiding in the wrong fortress does. When trouble comes, do you run to other people? Do you hide in the fortress of Netflix? Do you run to alcohol? Do you hide in the busyness of a work schedule? The reality is that we all run and we all hide, but there's only one safe place.*
>
> *The Lord is the world's most reliable stronghold. He has the power to protect you, and he has the grace to restore your soul. He gives strength to the weary and returns the joy of the broken."* [1]

How are things with you right now? Do you feel vulnerable and exposed? Are you afraid to let others see who you really are? I get it. The world can be a crazy place. But you're not alone. He is your shelter.

Rest in the shelter that the Cross provides. Rejoice in God's radical love for you. Trust that your standing with Him has nothing to do with what you do or have done. Believe in Him and walk in the newness of life. Allow the good news of unconditional forgiveness to give you a sense of relief. And know that nothing can change His love for you.

You don't need any other shelter today. And you are safe in His arms.

a prayer for today

Lord, it's so easy to get caught in the trap of comparison. I pray that you'll help me to not compare myself to those around me. Keep me from feeling "less than" when I see how put together others seem to be. But, Lord, keep me from feeling better about myself when I see the struggles that others face. Remind me today that my identity is anchored in who YOU say that I am. And may that be enough…

34

Meet Me Halfway?

We all love trite clichés like "Two are better than one!" or "If we each pull part of the load, we can carry the whole thing!" I think that there's actually a part of us that enjoys the idea that there is something for us to do, as long as someone else comes alongside us pulling their share of the weight. "Doing" makes us feel like we've accomplished something when we have finished.

Often we look at the sin and messiness in our lives and think, "Wow, this is awful! I need a little help to clean this mess up!" So we turn to Jesus and we ask Him to "come into our lives" and help us to clean up. On the surface this sounds good, but it doesn't in any way reflect what the Bible describes.

Amazingly, if you Google "Jesus Life Coach", you will find thousands of articles, resources and blogs that affirm that what you and I need is simply A LITTLE HELP. These well-meaning folks believe that what we are desperate for is an advisor who helps when we ask, but doesn't butt in when we don't need Him. He's a non-intrusive guru who simply coaches us through the difficult battle we have with sin.

Often, people come to Jesus asking Him for a little help. In Matthew, Jesus was asked for some help and He gave much more.

"Jesus climbed into a boat and went back across the lake to his own town. Some people brought to him a paralyzed man on a mat. Seeing their faith, Jesus said to the paralyzed man, "Be encouraged, my child! Your sins are forgiven." Matthew 9:1-2 NLT

What a moment! This paralyzed man was brought to Jesus because he had a problem. He couldn't walk. His friends had one goal in bringing him to Christ: Get him walking!

Jesus knew that this man had a much greater need. His paralysis was not his problem. His SIN was the problem! Jesus cut to the chase and did more than help him walk. The Son of God looked this man in the eye and pronounced the forgiveness of his sin.

You see, we need more than a coach, helper, adviser or leader. We need a SAVIOR! Our sin problem is so awful that it has separated us from God. We sinners are worthy of judgment and condemnation. We think we need help in finding a life of purpose and meaning and Jesus says, "You've got much bigger problems! That's why I came to Earth."

If you look at your life thinking that with a little help from God you can fulfill your life's purpose, you're missing it. Jesus did not die on a cross to do His part, leaving the rest up to you. He didn't do MOST of the work. He did it all, leaving nothing for you and me to do. The redemption work was accomplished by Him 100%. We don't meet Him halfway. He meets us…in the mud, the weeds and the slums. That's where sin has put us.

We have become bottom-dwellers. And Jesus is a bottom-feeder who meets us in the dark and ugly place.

You don't have to show initiative and resolve in order to get His attention. He's waiting for you to call His name today. He's already done all the work. There's nothing left for you to do except receive His loving and gracious gift of salvation. His grace is all you need. Leave your promises, your vows, and your best intentions behind. Allow Jesus to raise your dead bones to life. He didn't come to make good people better. He came to make dead people alive!

But some of us have a hard time with the idea that we don't bring anything to the salvation table. We want to contribute and feel like we're doing our part. No one wants to be a freeloader, right? Well, the reality of the Gospel upends the idea that we bring our promises, intentions and commitments to Him. It sounds like the American way where we say there is no free lunch! But we who are in Christ can now be seated at the banquet table knowing we did absolutely nothing to earn our seat.

And because His grace covers all your failure and rebellion, you can walk in the forgiveness that only His blood could purchase for you. If you are His, you have everything! You and I need more than a life coach. Thank you, Jesus, for being our Savior!

a prayer for today

God, you have promised to lead and guide me and in my heart. I want that. But I will be tempted to settle for my own direction for my life today. I very well may doubt that you're all that interested in my little life. Remind me in lots of ways, Lord, that you're here. I'm thick-headed so I'll need a lot of reminders. Thanks that my wandering heart doesn't frustrate you. Thank you for promising to never leave me, even when I leave you. Keep me today, God...

35

The Aggressive Pursuer

In the book of John we read:

"I am the good shepherd. The good shepherd sacrifices his life for the sheep. A hired hand will run when he sees a wolf coming. He will abandon the sheep because they don't belong to him and he isn't their shepherd. And so the wolf attacks them and scatters the flock. The hired hand runs away because he's working only for the money and doesn't really care about the sheep. I am the good shepherd; I know my own sheep, and they know me, just as my Father knows me and I know the Father. So I sacrifice my life for the sheep. I have other sheep, too, that are not in this sheepfold. I must bring them also. They will listen to my voice, and there will be one flock with one shepherd." John 10:11-16 NLT

And in Matthew:

"If a man has a hundred sheep and one of them wanders away, what will he do? Won't he leave the ninety-nine others on the hills and go out to search for the one that is lost? And if he finds it, I tell you the truth, he will rejoice over it more than over the ninety-nine that didn't wander away! In the same way, it is not my heavenly Father's will that even one of these little ones should perish." Matthew 18:12-14 NLT

I am not a farmer or rancher, but there are a few things I know about sheep. They are not very smart. They are prone to wander off from the group.

And they don't necessarily understand danger. Because these things are true, the job of a shepherd is really important. Kind of like managing a group of four-year-olds on a hike through the woods!

Sadly, you and I are a lot like sheep. Sin has rendered us less than able to navigate life on the straight and narrow. Like the great hymn says, "Prone to wander, Lord, I feel it. Prone to leave the God I love." Think about that for a second. Even though we know better – even though we've heard the truth of Jesus and His love, we wander from Him nonetheless.

But the Bible tells us that the Good Shepherd consistently pursues us when we stray. And as my brother-in-law puts it, he lovingly pursues us like a lion chases after a zebra!

In the movie, "The Fugitive", Federal Marshal Samuel Gerard hunts down escaped convict Richard Kimball. He is relentless. His whole life becomes focused on the pursuit and capture of the fugitive. He wants to bring this man to justice. His is almost an obsession. He wants to put Dr. Richard Kimball in prison for murdering his wife.

But Jesus is different. His pursuit is passionate and even aggressive. But it is loving and fueled by a desire to save, not to exact justice. He chases after us in the same way I would chase after one of my own children if they were lost. If they had gone astray, I'd make my whole life about finding them.

My brother-in-law, Ed Nugent, points to the words of Psalm 23 where David writes, "Surely goodness and mercy shall FOLLOW me all the days of my life..." The word "follow" has strong implications. It describes a predatory, yet loving pursuit. That's tough for us to wrap our brains around. The aggressive love of Jesus pursues the wanderers – you and me – and offers us relief instead of condemnation.

His pursuit offers rest and comfort instead of judgment and finger-pointing. And those words, "all the days of my life" are so very important. God will never tire of our wandering. He will never throw His hands in the air and cast us aside for messing up one too many times. He will never put limits on His grace.

Tullian Tchividjian is one of my "grace heroes" and he says this about the God who pursues us with His grace:

> *"Grace is love that seeks you out when you have nothing to give in return. Grace is love coming at you that has nothing to do with you. Grace is being loved when you are unlovable...."* [1]

Jesus the pursuer is chasing you...with love. He is pursuing you...with grace. He won't quit looking for you until you have once again tasted of His mercy. The Good Shepherd loves you and wants to give you more than just another chance. He wants to give sweet relief and rest for the weary. He will welcome you into His loving arms today. And if you're wandering now, know that the "Hound of Heaven" pursues you with His relentless and never-ending love. Your sin no longer disqualifies you from the salvation that Jesus gives. Trust in Him. He loves you more than anyone ever has or ever could. Receive His love and know that it comes with no strings attached.

a prayer for today

God, I confess to you now that I want to be lord of my own life a lot of the time. I fail to trust you and your plan for my life, even though I know better. Forgive me, please, for me wanting to be the king of my own world. And, Lord, please remind me in lots of ways today that Jesus has won for me your total acceptance. Thank you for not getting tired of my act. Thank you for loving this messy child of yours.

36

"You Can't Handle The Truth!"

It's possibly one of the most memorable movie lines of all time. Jack Nicholson, in the witness chair fires back at Tom Cruise who interrogates him, shouting, "You can't HANDLE the truth!" This courtroom exchange is one of the reasons I love "A Few Good Men".

The reality is that most of us can't handle the truth about ourselves. We don't want to know how bad we really are. Instead, we look to those who will build us up, telling us about a version of ourselves that we like. When we go to church, deep down we hope the pastor tells us that we can be all God wants us to be with just a little help from Jesus.

The Bible diagnoses our sin condition and it's truth that some of us can't handle at all:

"Since they thought it foolish to acknowledge God, he abandoned them to their foolish thinking and let them do things that should never be done. Their lives became full of every kind of wickedness, sin, greed, hate, envy, murder, quarreling, deception, malicious behavior, and gossip. They are backstabbers, haters of God, insolent, proud, and boastful. They invent new ways of sinning, and they disobey their parents. They refuse to understand, break their promises, are heartless, and have no mercy. They know God's justice requires that those who do these things deserve to die, yet they do them anyway. Worse yet, they encourage others to do them, too." Romans 1:28-32 NLT

This horrible description is the absolute truth about every man and woman who has ever lived (except Jesus). Our sin problem is way bigger than any of us really wants to admit. We're told by our family, our friends, our teachers and our co-workers that we're good people! A few flaws, yes, but we're generally pretty good!

The Bible has something different to say. It declares in no uncertain terms that we are way worse off that we could ever imagine. Our wretchedness is so over-the-top that it literally makes God sick! Later in Romans we read that "the wages of sin is death." Yikes!! Our sin-sickness has gotten us to a place we don't want to be. We really are lost! It looks like there is no hope for mankind.

But in Ephesians we find out that God, the Judge, delights to show mercy to wretched sinners like you and me.

"Once you were dead because of your disobedience and your many sins. You used to live in sin, just like the rest of the world, obeying the devil—the commander of the powers in the unseen world. He is the spirit at work in the hearts of those who refuse to obey God. All of us used to live that way, following the passionate desires and inclinations of our sinful nature. By our very nature we were subject to God's anger, just like everyone else. But God is so rich in mercy, and he loved us so much, that even though we were dead

because of our sins, he gave us life when he raised Christ from the dead. (It is only by God's grace that you have been saved!)" Ephesians 2: 1-5 NLT

The merciful God sent His Son Jesus to bear the burden of our sin. He meets us, not in the middle, but at the bottom! We bring nothing to Him except our sin and skepticism, and He washes us clean by His blood, never to be counted as guilty ever again. What an exchange.

Yes, we deserve His condemnation, but for those of us who are in Christ, we live in the freedom that the Gospel provides.

Jesus was already judged guilty on our behalf. And there will be no second trial!!! That's a hard thing for folks like us to wrap our brains around. It's difficult to accept that this is true. In our heads we might believe it, but to rest our hearts in His finished work – that's a different story.

Before the Gospel will sound like really good news, we must first be confronted with the reality of our awful sin. The bad news MUST come first. Otherwise, we look at our "goodness" and try to add a little Jesus to it to make us better. If that's how you "came to faith", it might be time to regroup and see what the Bible says about your sin condition. Then and only then, will God's grace be truly amazing.

If Wikileaks could hack my thoughts and share them with the world, I'd get kicked out of my house, asked to leave my church, taken off the air on Christian radio, and left friendless to find my way. Thankfully, Jesus has taken full and final responsibility for all of my sin - even the stuff I'm not aware of. My brokenness is very real, but so is His radical grace for messed up guys like me. He loves me and there's nothing I can do to stop it...

You can't handle the truth, and neither can I. But Jesus knows the whole truth about us, and He loves us with a love that never ends. And His love is not contingent on our love reciprocated.

One writer asked this question on Twitter: If you were standing at the altar getting married to the one you love and you knew that they would be unfaithful to you during the entire life of your marriage, would you go through with the wedding? Jesus did. We are His bride and though we be wildly unfaithful, He pledges His love for us

Mind-blowing good news....

a prayer for today

Lord, I need you today. Help to be loving and gracious when I interact with those whose opinions and passions are opposed to mine. I am so good at being judgmental and I need your help, God, to change. Please do a work in me today. Remind me of your kind and patient and generous love for broken people like me. And help me to reflect that love as I will encounter others who look at life from a different perspective than I do. Help me to not be a jerk today...

37

Jesus Is NOT "The Reason For The Season"!

I have an acquaintance who went into a bank a few weeks before Christmas to deposit some checks. This was a small town and she had been inside that bank hundreds of times over the years. This particular time she noticed a big Christmas tree displayed in the lobby and lots of candy canes and tinsel decorating the place. There was a plastic Santa standing outside one of the offices, too. This bothered her.

When it was her turn, she handed the teller the checks to be deposited and smiled politely. It was Christmastime, after all. When the teller finished the transaction, she handed the woman a receipt and sweetly said, "Happy Holidays!" The woman – my acquaintance - was incensed!! Looking back, I wonder if she regrets making the kind of scene she made.

"What is with you all? Look at all this Christmas stuff that you've put everywhere! Where is Jesus??? How about a nativity scene or an angel or something? I can't tell you how offended I am right now. Come on! Don't you know that Jesus is the reason for the season???"

She stormed out the door and didn't go back inside that bank for months.

Maybe you've seen the "Christmas Wars" play out in your church or school – maybe even your workplace.

And Lord knows, Christian bookstores work very hard to remind you that Jesus is the reason for the season! It's kind of their job, I guess. Too much Rudolph and not enough Jesus is going to ruin everything, right!

Well, I came to an important conclusion recently and you might not like it. You see, I discovered in, of all places the Bible, that Jesus is most certainly NOT the reason for the season.

I am. You are. We are.

Jesus had been spotted at the homes of some of the "sinners" in town and church leaders didn't like it very much:

Later, Levi invited Jesus and his disciples to his home as dinner guests, along with many tax collectors and other disreputable sinners. (There were many people of this kind among Jesus' followers.) But when the teachers of religious law who were Pharisees saw him eating with tax collectors and other sinners, they asked his disciples, "Why does he eat with such scum?" When Jesus heard this, he told them, "Healthy people don't need a doctor—sick people do. I have come to call not those who think they are righteous, but those who know they are sinners." Mark 2:15-17 NLT

Jesus was not on some heavenly reconnaissance mission to check in on us – to make sure things on Earth were going ok. He didn't come to be Yoda for you and me who simply needed a little guidance. He didn't come shake hands and reward the most righteous with a cruise or some extra frequent flier miles. He came to live and to die!

Jesus left His heavenly home because of the mess that sin had created in the lives of broken and messed up people. He came, not to show us how to live, but to live the life we couldn't live, meeting all of God's demands. It was our failure to even come close to loving God with all our heart, soul, mind and strength that made His arrival in the manger necessary.

And it was our sin that made death and resurrection His mission on Earth. He took our sin upon himself and gave us the full credit for the perfect life He lived. WE WERE THE REASON! Jesus is not the reason for the season. I am the reason He came. You were the reason He came. And in His arrival came hope for a broken world. In that barn in Bethlehem a Saviour was born. He came for you and me and His eyes were fixed on His mission.

John Piper says it quite clearly:

> *"The reason we need a ransom to be paid for us is that we have sold ourselves into sin and have been alienated from a holy God. When Jesus gave his life as a ransom, our slave masters, sin and death and the devil, had to give up their claim on us. And the result was that we could be adopted into the family of God."* [1]

Here's a really neat truth, my friend. If you were the only broken sinner in the world, He would have come for you. He loves you that much! Do you believe His promise to you? If you do, nothing that you do today can mess this up. Rest in the Gospel today…

a prayer for today

God, I want to be a faithful follower today. But sometimes my faith is weak. I want to be committed to you today. But my track record would indicate that I'm pretty flaky and I fail at this more than I want to admit. But you are faithful! Your are committed to me!! May I rest in that today. Lord, I pray that your love for me would captivate my heart so powerfully that I would live my life in gratitude for what you've done to rescue this sinner.

38

"Oh, Come On, You're Not That Bad..."

Like I've said before, I am a recovering alcoholic.

I've struggled with my inability to manage my drinking for thirteen years. It will be a lifelong struggle, I can promise you. At my worst point, I was drinking 8-10 glasses of wine each afternoon/evening. Sometimes it was five or six glasses with a few healthy swigs of whiskey, rum or vodka. I drank myself to sleep thousands of nights. Yet, few people knew. No one REALLY knew how unmanageable my life had become.

A few well-meaning people who I confided in said things like, "Oh, Jeff – come on you're not that bad. Just slow down a little bit or stop altogether. You're fine." They couldn't have been more wrong. I was in a downward spiral that would result in nothing good for me. I needed more than a helping hand. I needed outside intervention.

My son, Tommy, has an autism spectrum disorder. We noticed some peculiarities at age two but didn't want to overreact. People told us, "No, he's fine! He'll grow out of this." We disagreed and pursued this with his pediatrician and later, a psychologist named Dr. Chris. We were told that we needed to take action in helping our son. We would have to reinvent ourselves as parents in order to help him learn and grow. To ignore the seriousness of this would be to fail our son. We didn't.

We want to be encouragers, don't we! When we can offer words of hope or relief, it makes us feel good. And doesn't the Bible tell us to be that way? And while painting a "glass half full" picture to someone else might be ok, I guess, when you and I deceive ourselves into thinking we're not that bad, we're on very dangerous ground.

"We are all infected and impure with sin. When we display our righteous deeds, they are nothing but filthy rags. Like autumn leaves, we wither and fall, and our sins sweep us away like the wind. Yet no one calls on your name or pleads with you for mercy. Therefore, you have turned away from us and turned us over to our sins." Isaiah 64:6-7

This is how the Bible diagnoses all of us. And read those words – it sounds pretty bad. It doesn't paint a pretty picture of our hearts and our attempts at being good, does it? These words are indicting! They are full of condemnation, which we deserve, because we are THAT BAD. Hard words to read. Not very positive, upbeat and encouraging.

Ray Ortlund tweeted this and it so resonated with me when I think about how truly bad I am:

> *"If 'total depravity' is real, then even our heroic moral stands can be infested with evil. We're left with *no* superiority. Hard to take."* [1]

And yet, the news is so good because of Jesus!

He took upon himself the sin of the world. Mankind's inability to meet the holy demands of a righteous God were met with Christ's sacrificial exchange on an old bloody Cross. But Jesus didn't just die for the idea of salvation. For Him it was personal. You see, it was for YOU that He came, lived, died and rose again. Your sin was so great that it required outside intervention. And Jesus paid for your sins – past, present and future.

The Law declares that we really ARE that bad. We are far worse than we think. Our rebellion shows itself every day in the things we do and leave undone. We were born into this world enemies of God.

But the wall that separates sinners from a holy God has been decimated by God's Son. By faith each one who believes undergoes a complete status change. No longer are we defined by our sin, our rebellion, or failures. Our identity is now anchored in who HE says we are. And He calls you His dearly-loved child.

The bad news of the Law has to break us. It must crush us. Otherwise we think we're pretty good people in need of a little help now and again. The Law humbles us and reveals our desperation. But the Gospel announces that Jesus has made everything right, now and forever!! The Good News really is sweet when it falls on the ears of broken and messed up people like us!

Today, let the reality of the Law do its job. Let it reveal your great need. Then, let the Gospel wash over you - it announces that because of Jesus, you will never ever experience the condemnation of God. Your Judgment Day has been moved from the future to the past. Boom!

a prayer for today

God, we will be tempted to look to many things that we hope will satisfy us today. Things that are much less than Jesus. That's who we are. We're "prone to wander". But because the Gospel is true, you will never kick us to the curb because of our wandering. You pursue us with a love that is bigger than we can comprehend. By your grace, you accept wanderers who are trusting in the finished work of your Son. This is good news for broken folks like me...thanks, Lord.

39
The Broken Ones Are Over There...

I talk to people all the time about brokenness and I can tell you, it makes some of them uncomfortable. You see, they don't see themselves as broken or messy or desperate at all. I probably offend them when I talk on the radio or from a pulpit about the one thing we all share in common: We are all broken.

It's easy to look "over THERE" to find the truly broken among us. The drug addicts, the serial philanderers, the violent criminals, the pathological and the weak. Those people are the broken ones, right? They've given the finger to anyone who tried to help them. They've used up all their chances. They won't take responsibility for their decisions and actions. They fail over and over again. Don't try to help them because they don't want to help themselves. And they'll get what's coming to them, that's for sure.

When I think of the people who fill that category, names like Charles Manson, Jim Jones, John Edwards, Ted Kacsinski, Terry Nichols, and a host of others currently in one kind of prison or another. We shake our heads at them. But in doing so, we expose a problem. You see, we are hypocrites.

In the book of Luke we read a story that cuts to the very heart of our hypocrisy.

"Two men went to the Temple to pray. One was a Pharisee, and the other was a despised tax collector. The Pharisee stood by himself and prayed this prayer: 'I thank you, God, that I am not like other people—cheaters, sinners, adulterers. I'm certainly not like that tax collector! I fast twice a week, and I give you a tenth of my income.'

"But the tax collector stood at a distance and dared not even lift his eyes to heaven as he prayed. Instead, he beat his chest in sorrow, saying, 'O God, be merciful to me, for I am a sinner.' I tell you, this sinner, not the Pharisee, returned home justified before God. For those who exalt themselves will be humbled, and those who humble themselves will be exalted." Luke 18:10-14 NLT

In case you were wondering, you and I are represented by the Pharisee. In our arrogance, we look at the "tax collectors" of the world and feel a sense of relief that we aren't as bad as them. Why would we beat our chest in sorrow over our sin when we honestly think we're doing pretty well. I mean, we make a few mistakes now and again, but we're not that broken, right?

It's sobering to see yourself in this story and realize that you're broken like everyone else. In God's economy, sin is sin and guilt is guilt. We are the broken ones. We stand right alongside the hookers, thieves, abortion doctors, rapists and everyone else in our guilt. The ground in front of the Cross is level. This news ought to stun us. The sting of God's expectations and our failure to meet them should hurt. We have failed miserably. The Bible says we deserve judgment, condemnation and death. Bad news for the broken ones…

This is where I have to confess that in my hypocrisy I am very good at justifying my own sin while condemning the sin of you and everyone else. It makes me feel just a little less broken, if I'm being honest. But the reality is this: I have so much "yuck" in my life that it sometimes leaves me feeling pretty rotten. And most of my broken mess is kept in the dark so that you won't be able to see it. But God sees it and He knows.

Sir Arthur Canon Doyle sent telegrams to five of his friends as a joke. The telegrams read:

"All has been discovered. Flee at once."

One of his friends upon receiving the note, packed up, moved away and was never heard from again. Apparently he had lots of "yuck" in his closet.

On the Cross, Jesus took full and final responsibility for our sin and brokenness. He bore the shame that we deserve to carry because of our failure to meet God's holy demands. He absorbed God's anger toward our sin once and for all. And we members of a huge club called "The League Of The Broken" can find rest and relief in the sweet words of the Gospel.

Here is the Bible's diagnosis of each one of us:

"God's light came into the world, but people loved the darkness more than the light, for their actions were evil." John 3:19 NLT

But here is God's promise to all who believe:

"Therefore, since we have been made right in God's sight by faith, we have peace with God because of what Jesus Christ our Lord has done for us. Because of our faith, Christ has brought us into this place of undeserved privilege where we now stand, and we confidently and joyfully look forward to sharing God's glory." Romans 5:1-2 NLT

We are the broken ones. All of us. And we are loved by God. All of us. Let that truth move you forward as you navigate your life today!

a prayer for today

God, I need you to remind me in lots of ways that my sin and brokenness is real. Not so that I'll be defeated and live in despair, but, rather, so that I will be reminded of what you did for me. You took full and final responsibility for my sin and have given me your perfect record as my own. May the keen awareness of my brokenness drive me to you, Lord, where I am certain to receive grace and mercy. And God, may that radical reality affect every relationship in my life today...

40

"That Camper You're Pulling Is Really Gonna Slow You Down!"

My wife's parents are easing into retirement. Their home is in Southwest Florida but much of their family and many of their friends are scattered across the country. So they have begun a new phase in life. In an effort to be light on their feet as they travel the nation, they are now "camper people". With their van they pull a camper that is like a little apartment on wheels!

This camper is fully-equipped. There is a bedroom, a kitchen, a bathroom and a living area, complete with flat screen TV. It's quite comfortable and they can set it up practically anywhere. It gives them the freedom to travel as they choose, yet it gives them a sense of "home" at the same time.

But there's a problem, you see.

While they motor down the Interstates of America, they can only go 57 mph because that camper is heavier than they anticipated. They have become right-lane people and it seems to take forever to get anywhere. That camper is absolutely slowing them down! It's holding them back. It forces them to spend more hours than they'd like getting to the next destination. I don't know how long the camper is going to be part of the family…

As you and I move forward in our lives having embraced the radical freedom that the Gospel gives, we have to be careful.

If we are not soaking in the truth of God's grace and mercy every day – if we are not preaching the Gospel to ourselves all the time – we can retreat back to our default. Do more, try harder. It can happen slowly over time and it can blur our Gospel vision. We can actually get to a place where we think that it was Jesus' blood and sweat that got me into God's good graces, but it will be my blood and sweat that keeps me there.

The burden that this creates can slow us down as we navigate through this life. Like my in-laws' camper, it can weigh us down and keep us from enjoying the sweet freedom that the Bible promises all who believe! And rather than being people whose burden has been lifted, we will become weary Christ-followers who just can't ever seem to get it done. And it will slow us down. It might even shut us down. We're trying to bear a load that Jesus has already taken. Why would we trade our freedom for that?

And yet, we find ourselves here again and again. I think it's because grace goes against everything that life tells us. It flies in the face of the American dream! It really sounds too good to be true. I wrote this book so that you and I will have yet another reminder that the Gospel really is true.

Listen to Paul's warning to the Galatians:

"Oh, foolish Galatians! Who has cast an evil spell on you? For the meaning of Jesus Christ's death was made as clear

to you as if you had seen a picture of his death on the cross. Let me ask you this one question: Did you receive the Holy Spirit by obeying the law of Moses? Of course not! You received the Spirit because you believed the message you heard about Christ. How foolish can you be? After starting your new lives in the Spirit, why are you now trying to become perfect by your own human effort? Have you experienced so much for nothing?

Surely it was not in vain, was it? I ask you again, does God give you the Holy Spirit and work miracles among you because you obey the law? Of course not! It is because you believe the message you heard about Christ." Galatians 3:1-5

Despite knowing the truth of the radical Gospel, these believers retreated into thinking that it was on them! They heard the truth, believed the truth, and now doubted the truth. They had forgotten the simple message of God's grace and mercy given to undeserving sinners. They thought that maybe there was something to be added to the Gospel. Or maybe they thought that the Gospel was like baby food and now they needed to get serious! Either way, Paul cries out to them, calling them back to the sweet news of Jesus' love and forgiveness to all who believe.

And I bet they read that letter from Paul over and over again, because they would certainly forget again. This side of heaven we will struggle to believe that he really loves us that much. We will struggle to accept the total and complete forgiveness that's ours because of the Cross. We're like thick-headed sheep.

Today, you will be tempted to pull the camper of guilt and doubt as you move from place to place. Don't believe the lie. What Jesus did was once and for all. His condemnation of sin will never touch you because Jesus took it! You were never meant to bear the load of all that. You're free!! Unhitch the camper and leave it by the side of the road. You don't need to pull that thing…

a prayer for today

Lord, when I look at my heart I struggle with what I see. My brokenness frustrates me because I want to be better. I want to get it right. And yet, I fail miserably to be all that I should be. BUT, you aren't frustrated with me. You don't look at my mess and shake your head. Instead, you love me extravagantly and you accept me fully because of the work of another. May the reality of Jesus love for me compel me to love and serve you today.

stuff i forgot to say...

After reading this book, one thing must be very clear to you: I am not some grace guru who gets it all perfectly. I feel like an infant when it comes to my understanding of Christ's work on our behalf. Grace confuses me sometimes. It can also seem too good to be true! Come on, you think so, too, right?

Years ago, the Holy Spirit turned the lights on inside my heart and mind and I began to taste the sweetness of the Gospel – the REAL Gospel. I always believed that Jesus died for my sins. I believed that He forgave me and cleansed me. But I struggled with the idea that surely there must be something left for me to do. There had to be at least a few strings because nothing is free, really.

My "grace awakening" wasn't simply a flash of instant understanding. It began a process that is still occurring in me. The more I soak in the finished work of Jesus, the more at peace I am. The more I believe the truth of the radical Gospel, the more I live under the banner that reads, "It Is Finished"! The more I can be honest about my brokenness before God and others, the more free I am because He came for broken and messed up people like Jeff. And you, too.

On the radio I talk a lot about grace. Some people wonder if I am able to talk about anything else. Those people make me smile because they raise a good question. And, no, why would I want to talk about anything but God's grace for undeserving people. In fact, on my tombstone, I wouldn't mind if below my name it said, "GOSPEL FIRE HYDRANT".

And like I've said a few times in this little book of mine, I'm not interested in a message of grace that produces deadness in our spiritual lives. Since experiencing my grace awakening, I've never wanted to serve the Lord with my life more! In the years that I have left on this planet, I want to tell the old, old story to anyone who will listen.

To the most broken among us I say, "I am with you." To the failures who read this book I say, "I am absolutely one of you and I have the track record to prove it!" And to the hurting and hopeless I say, "Jesus loves you and gave himself for you. Only He can satisfy you."

You might have read this book and thought that I just don't get it. Fair enough, my friend. Maybe I don't get it. But as Bono says, "The reason I talk about grace so much is that I'm depending on it!"

If you've grown up in a religious tradition that brought rules, expectations and guilt your way, I pray that Say Grace has been like a cool drink of water on a very hot day. If your church or pastor beat you up with the Law and left you feeling like a very bad Christian, my hope is that Say Grace has convinced you that there is a better way – a truer way.

The Gospel brings sweet relief to sinners who know that they are far worse than they even know. Soak in it and let it reorient your heart and mind.

Because I work in Christian radio, some people think that I should be an example to others. I ask them, "An example of what?" They usually are implying that I should represent some kind of spiritual maturity demonstrated by my better living. They think that my spiritual wisdom should run high and my struggles should be kept quiet.

Well, I want to be an example. I want to be an ambassador of the Gospel. I want to be transparent about my brokenness and struggle.

I want to confess my deep sin-sickness to the world because – wait for it – JESUS LOVES ME!!! He knows me and He loves me! He took my sin with Him to the Cross and He has given me His righteousness! I want to represent THAT kind of Jesus – the REAL Jesus...

I hope that this book has been sweet news for people who have failed and fallen – that's all of us.

I hope that the words on these pages bring relief for people with bad reputations and spotty records. The Gospel doesn't sound like good news until the reality of our sin and brokenness is real to us. I hope the Law continues to break you. And I hope the reality of your sin drives you to the One who loves rotten sinners. His name is Jesus and this book is about Him.

I also hope that Say Grace inspires discussions at Bible studies and small groups. The message of radical grace usually creates strong feelings. If you are one of those folks who "get it", don't steamroll over those who are not yet at a place where this kind of grace has taken root. We can make a legalism out of grace if we're not careful, you know.

Some people ask me if I will write another book one day. I don't know. I am considering the idea. I have to grow in grace a little first. But if I die tomorrow, Say Grace is my heart's cry to the world. If I am to be known for anything, other than my sin and the wreckage I've left behind, I want to be known for this truth expressed on every page of the book:

"Grace, grace, God's grace – grace that will pardon and cleanse within. Grace, grace, God's grace – grace that is greater than all my sin"…

sources

Chapter One:
1. https://www.facebook.com/ragamuffingospel/posts/388456071190

Chapter Four:
2. https://www.keylife.org/articles/radical-freedom

Chapter Six:
3. https://www.thegospelcoalition.org/article/the-myth-of-moral-superiority – Jen Pollock Michel
4. https://jdgreear.com/blog/three-reasons-you-cant-make-a-deal-with-god/- J.D. Greear

Chapter Seven:
5. Phillip Yancey, Facebook post, September 3, 2014
6. Matt Chandler http://theresurgence.com/2013/01/29/we-must-move-in-grace

Chapter Eight:
7. "Only Grace", Matthew West and Kenny Greenberg, "History" 2005, Universal South Records

Chapter Nine:
8. "Texas Band Emphasizes Life-Changing Message" https://www.baptiststandard.com/news/faith-culture/16312-texas-band-emphasizes-life-changing-message

Chapter Ten:

9. "Will God Forgive Me For Having An Abortion?", Chad Bird, http://www.chadbird.com/blog/2016/1/24/will-god-forgive-me-for-having-an-abortion
10. "Sanctifying Success Is The Lord's", Jared C. Wilson, https://blogs.thegospelcoalition.org/gospeldrivenchurch/2014/05/21/sanctifying-success-is-the-lords/

Chapter Eleven:

11. "You Can't Move Beyond The Gospel", Benjamin Warfield, http://www.bloggingtheologically.com/2010/03/05/bb-warfield-christian-you-cant-move-beyond-the-gospel/

Chapter Twelve:

12. Lutheran Anglicans, Robert Capon, https://lutherananglican.com/the-capon-corner/

Chapter Thirteen:

13. LIBERATE 2013, Zac Hicks, zachicks.com
14. "Do You Still Want To Be Like Mike?", Matt Smethurst, https://www.thegospelcoalition.org/article/when-greatness-meets-emptiness-michael-jordan-at-50

Chapter Fifteen:

15. "Power In Preaching: Delight", Ray Ortlund, November 2009, http://themelios.thegospelcoalition.org/article/power-in-preaching-delight-2-corinthians-12110-part-3-of-3

Chapter Sixteen:

16. "Reminiscing", Graeham Goble, EMI 1978
17. Michael Horton on Twitter, https://twitter.com/michaelhorton_/status/718845990665478146

Chapter Seventeen:

18. Nick Lannon on Twitter, @nicklannon

Chapter Eighteen:

19. "Motivations For Obedience", Matt Chandler, http://www.tvcresources.net/resource-library/sermons/motivations-for-obedience
20. "How Good Is Good Enough?", Ross Lester, http://www.acts29.com/psalm-15/

Chapter Nineteen:

21. "Overwhelmed With God's Mercy, Grace and Hope", Scotty Smith, https://blogs.thegospelcoalition.org/scottysmith/2017/05/21/overwhelmed-with-gods-mercy-grace-and-hope/

Chapter Twenty-One:

22. https://blogs.thegospelcoalition.org/justintaylor/2010/05/26/an-interview-with-tullian-tchividjian-on-gospel-and-law/

Chapter Twenty-Two:

23. "He Is Not The God Of Second Chances, Aaron Wilson, https://www.thegospelcoalition.org/article/he-is-not-the-god-of-second-chances

Chapter Twenty-Three:

24. "The Danger Of Seeking Your Dream Church", Brian Borgman, https://www.thegospelcoalition.org/article/the-danger-of-seeking-your-dream-church

Chapter Twenty-Four:

25. "Theology Of Glory Vs. Theology Of The Cross", Tullian Tchividjian, http://www.christianpost.com/news/theology-of-glory-vs-theology-of-the-cross-78119/
26. "What Makes A Gospel-Centered Church", Ray Ortlund, http://www.epm.org/blog/2017/Mar/17/gospel-centered-church

Chapter Twenty-Six:

27. "Your Own Personal Jesus", John Suk, http://www.christianitytoday.com/pastors/2006/march-online-only/your-own-personal-jesus-is-language-of-personal.html

Chapter Twenty-Seven:

28. "Four Ways To Win The Battle Against Busyness", J.D. Greear, https://www.thegospelcoalition.org/article/4-ways-to-win-the-battle-against-busyness

Chapter Twenty-Eight:

https://www.brainyquote.com/quotes/keywords/reputation.html

Chapter Twenty-Nine:

29. In The Grip Of Grace, Bryan Chapell, Grand Rapids: Baker, 1992

Chapter Thirty:

30. Robert Kolb and Charles P. Arand, The Genius of Luther's Theology: A Wittenberg Way of Thinking for the Contemporary Church (Grand Rapids, MI: Baker Academic, 2008), 124-128.

Chapter Thirty-One:

31. http://daddy4ms.blogspot.com/2016/03/tweets-and-more-tweets.html

Chapter Thirty-Two:

32. Gavin Ortlund http://www.cslewisinstitute.org/The_Defiance_of_Grace_in_the_Ministry_of_Jesus_FullArticle
33. https://www.bestquotecollection.com/quote/jerry-bridges/605890

Chapter Thirty-Three:

34. "Run And Hide", Paul David Tripp, http://www.paultripp.com/ViewMail.aspx?mmid=9a5g70489289a5g7008

Chapter Thirty-Five:

35. Tullian Tchividjian on Twitter. https://twitter.com/tulliant/status/440513051889262592

Chapter Thirty-Six:

36. "Jesus Is For Sinners", Chad West,
https://www.keylife.org/articles/jesus-is-for-sinners1

Chapter Thirty-Seven:

37. "Why The Son Of God Came Into The World", John Piper,
http://www.desiringgod.org/messages/why-the-son-of-god-came-into-the-world

Chapter Thirty-Eight:

38. Ray Ortlund on Twitter.
https://twitter.com/rayortlund/status/770426581475098626

Meet Jeff Taylor Sandnes:

Jeff is best-known as one-half of the morning duo "Jeff & Rebecca" on KCBI-FM in Dallas-Ft. Worth. He brings a combination of transparency and laughs to the radio and along with Rebecca Carrell, theirs has been one of the fastest-growing morning shows in the DFW Metroplex. You can listen using the free KCBI app or at kcbi.org. Monday-Friday, 5:30-8:30AM CT.

KCBI is a grateful recipient of the 2017 Radio "Station Of The Year" award given by the National Religious Broadcasters.

Prior to arriving in Texas, Jeff did mornings on WAY-FM in Southwest Florida. As the General Manager, he led the ministry in Ft. Myers/Naples for over 15 years. Teaming with Joy Summers, "Jeff & Joy" was a top-rated morning show in Southwest Florida and was soon syndicated to stations in Denver and Portland.

WAY-FM received "Station Of The Year" honors from the Gospel Music Association in 2010.

Jeff has a passion for the Gospel and believes in the message of God's radical grace for broken and messed up people like you and me. He has brought this message to gatherings all across the country and served as one of the chaplains of the World Champion Boston Red Sox.

In 1999, Jeff wrote his first book, LIFE SUPPORT: A Prescription For Prolonging The Life Of Your Youth Worker. It has been a help to many congregations that want to keep good youth ministry people from leaving too quickly.

A youth ministry veteran of more than a decade, Jeff has served churches in Washington, Minnesota, Florida and New York. He believes that the good news really does set us free from the bondage of what many call "performancism". It's a message that the church needs to hear now more than ever. He believes that the Law and the Gospel go hand in hand and need to live together.

Jeff is a graduate of The King's College and was named 2016 "Alumnus Of The Year". He has also studied at Fuller Seminary and Lutheran Brethren Seminary.

You can find him on the web at iambroken.org.

Jeff is available to speak at your church, conference or other gathering. Email him at jeff@iambroken.org

Jeff is husband to Larisa and father to Tommy and Kate. They are his primary ministry and are tremendous grace-givers. His wife would tell you that he has the diet of an 11-year-old boy and hasn't met a burger he didn't like. He's also a very proud Norwegian!

That's about it…